RADICAL

Transforming People and Businesses Through
Powerful Coaching Conversations

Nic Oliver

Foreword by Daniel Wagner

First published in 2013 in Great Britain by Westbrook Publishing.

Copyright © 2013 by Nic Oliver, All Rights Reserved.

ISBN-13: 978-1493683314 / ISBN-10: 1493683314

Nic Oliver has asserted his right under the Copyright, Designs and Patents Act 1988 to be identified as the author of this work. No part of this book may be used or reproduced, stored in a retrieval system or transmitted in any form or by any means, electronically, mechanically, through photocopying, recording, scanning or otherwise except as permitted by the Copyright, Designs and Patents Act 1988, without either the prior written permission of the publisher or the author.

This book is sold subject to the condition that it shall not, by way of trade or otherwise, be lent, resold, hired out, or otherwise circulated without the publisher or author's prior consent in any form of binding or cover other than that in which it is published and without a similar condition, including this condition, being imposed on the subsequent purchaser.

Limit of Liability/Disclaimer of Warranty:
The facts, circumstances and contact details provided by the contributors was believed to be correct at the time of publication but may have changed since. While the publisher and author have used their best efforts in preparing this book, they make no representations or warranties with respect to the accuracy or completeness of the contents of this book and specifically disclaim any implied warranties of merchantability or fitness for a particular purpose.

The advice and strategies contained herein may not be suitable for your situation. If in doubt, you are advised to take professional advice. Neither the publisher nor author shall be liable for any personal loss, loss of profit or any other commercial damages, including but not limited to special, incidental, consequential or other damages.

Book cover design, formatting and publishing by Chrystel Melhuish, Owner of Plum Design & Publishing Ltd

DEDICATION

This book is dedicated to two people:

Firstly to my father-in-law who has recently won the toughest of mental challenges, overcoming stage 4 lung cancer and confounding the medical experts in the process. A powerful demonstration of what can be done!

Secondly, to my darling wife Mathilda, for your unconditional love and support. This book would not have been possible without you. It's an honor, and great fun, to share my life with you!

CONTENTS

Acknowledgements 1

Foreword 3

What others have written about Radical Coaching 5

Introduction 1

:: Part 1 :: 9

Chapter 1: Coaching 9

Chapter 2: Twelve Coaching Myths 13

Chapter 3: Radical Coaching 31

Chapter 4: Radical Business Coaching 37

Chapter 5: The Radical Coaching Conversation 39

Chapter 6: Radical Coaching Premises 43

Chapter 7: Hara Point Exercise 47

Chapter 8: Servant Leadership in Radical Coaching 51

Chapter 9: Coaching from Spirit 57

Chapter 10: Perception - The Power of Thought 63

Chapter 11: Reframing your Perception 73

Chapter 12: Self Limiting Frames 85

Chapter 13: The Three Principles 95

Chapter 14: The Potential of the Three Principles in Radical Coaching 105

Chapter 15: Positive Psychology – The Power of Emotions 111

Chapter 16: The Potential of Positive Psychology in Radical Coaching 121

Chapter 17: Emotional Intelligence 125

Chapter 18: The Importance of Emotional Intelligence in Radical Coaching 131

Chapter 19: Emotional Intelligence Exercise 139

Chapter 20: Appreciative Enquiry – The Power of Words 141

Chapter 21: The Potential of Appreciative Inquiry in Radical Coaching 159

Quick Comparison 163

:: Part 2 :: **165**

Introduction to Part 2 165

Chapter 22: Your Personal Coaching Motives 167

Chapter 23: Radical Coaching Model 185

Chapter 24: The Coaching Ladder 195

Chapter 25: The Art of Great Conversations 199

Chapter 26: The Initial Coaching Conversation 211

Chapter 27: Values 215

Chapter 28: Powerful Goals 219

:: Part 3 :: **223**

Introduction to Part 3 223

Chapter 29: The Conventional Approach to Marketing 225

Chapter 30: Building your Radical Coaching Business – Your Business PRISM 233

Chapter 31: PRISM Shortlist 241

Chapter 32: Strategic Offering Funnel 245

Chapter 33: The Dangers of Free Sessions 247

Chapter 34: Sales Process 249

Chapter 35: The 'Prosperous Coach' Method 251

Epilogue 253

Annex - The Fears That Hold us Back 255

Bibliography 263

ACKNOWLEDGMENTS

My heartfelt thanks to those who have influenced my coaching, and the development of Radical Coaching. I have been influenced by so many people as I read a lot but in particular, I want to thank Rich Litvin, Steve Chandler, Christian Mickelsen, Sydney Banks, Richard Bandler, Serge King and Daniel Wagner of the Expert Success Formula.

Thanks to my children Katherine and Matthew for being my greatest teachers.

Thanks also to Sophie Mercier and to Paramita who kept nagging me to do fewer training courses and more coaching. I got the message, eventually!

More thanks are due to Matthieu Kleinschmager, Dominika Nowak and the rest of the OD team in the European Commission – you have a message that your world needs to hear and I'm proud to play a small part in delivering it.

Many thanks to Claudia Ritter for your quiet thoughtfulness and encouragement during all of those evening meals in Brussels.

Thanks also to 'The Brussels gang' of consultants for the evenings spent putting the training and coaching worlds to rights – Ralph Houston, Peter Dunne, Pete Willis, John Parr, Michael DeToro, Sally Holley.

Thank you to Anita Sheehan for introducing me to Appreciative Inquiry.

Finally, a big thank you to Rene Julyan for your amazing research skills and writing. I could not have done this without your help. Good luck with the birth of your first baby.

FOREWORD

I was flattered when Nic asked me to write the introduction to his book "Radical Coaching". Nic is a highly experienced coach and trainer and his network includes some of the world's top experts from the world of coaching, consulting and training.

So to be chosen to put a few meaningful words at the beginning of his first book is a privilege. What Nic has achieved in this book is what most new coaching books fail to achieve. Through his extensive research, he not just builds on the greats of the past but develops these approaches with unique insights from his own personal and business life. His myriad of experiences create a coaching and training approach which is not only holistic and spiritual, but proves highly effective in a wide range of applications - from life to business coaching and from sports and wealth coaching to clinical therapy.

Nic starts out with busting some of the core coaching myths and then moves on to a potted history and definition of coaching from his own experience. I was fascinated and have not before read some of the information shared with such brevity and clarity.

From the 'Servant Leadership' model to the 'Three Principles' and from using 'Positive Psychology' to 'Emotional Intelligence' and more, Nic explains in simple to understand language, why he has chosen to build on these approaches and then suggests their practical applications in the Radical Coaching approach.

This book would already be a great book if Nic had left it at this point. But Nic goes further: He suggests powerful exercises for new and existing coaches to find their true coaching purpose and also helps them build successful coaching businesses. These chapters include some of the advanced marketing strategies and concepts that I teach in Expert Success and the Expert Success Academy.

Nic also provides powerful conversation templates and coaching questions that can be used immediately should you wish to apply the Radical Coaching model to your coaching practice.

It is a great pleasure to work with Nic and help him grow his business to help him spread the powerful message of Radical Coaching. Radical Coaching pursues the worthwhile goal to re-establish a person's balance and lead him to exploit his full potential leading to more happiness and fulfillment.

What higher goal could one pursue?

I urge you to read Nic's book, complete the exercises and take your learnings from Radical Coaching to the world. It will lead you to more insights and fulfillment.

To Your Success,
Daniel Wagner, Expert Success Academy

WHAT OTHERS HAVE WRITTEN ABOUT RADICAL COACHING

"Nic's book is a beautiful synthesis of the best coaching and leadership practices around. He is drawing both from the latest findings in Western psychology and biology as well as from traditional Eastern thought. This utterly readable and lucid book is both a practical and spiritual guide to personal development and to growing a coaching business. Rare is the book where you can find such value in virtually every sentence. It will leave you energized and transformed. Nic truly succeeded in writing 'a book that unlocks the traffic jam in everybody's head' (John Updike)."

Anita Sheehan, Leadership Coach and Appreciative Inquiry Facilitator.

:::::

"The Radical Coach is a refreshing change amongst the confusion that can surround coaching information, techniques and strategies. Nic has managed to share his own personal experience and translate that into language that is not only inspiring but also down to earth and makes complete sense.

It's the common sense approach to coaching that succinctly takes the reader on a journey through the various approaches to coaching people and captures the essence of each. He then allows the reader to interpret in a way that is workable and of practical benefit. Whether you are a new coach or old hat at it, this book will provide you with a viewpoint that will offer you practical support and also add to your toolkit to support both your clients and your own personal development.

Michelle Atkin, Conversations that Connect

:::::

"Nic has brilliantly captured and explained the importance of using your own truly unique coaching tool - your intuition - to bring life and true spirit to your coaching sessions. Radical Coaching bucks the trend of process driven coaching and encourages heartfelt coaching. The techniques and guidance in the book, I feel, will allow the clients to be true to themselves and allow the coaches to be more connected and present with themselves and their clients. Fabulous Book Nic, it's like written permission to be a different breed of coach and follow your heart. I've already used several of the techniques with success and I can't wait to see the Radical Coaching Academy evolve."

Liz Brown, Coach and Owner of www.liz-brown.net

INTRODUCTION

This is a different type of coaching book – deliberately so. A lot of books have been written about coaching skills and I certainly don't want to add another one that rehashes the same content. However, to say it is different is a bit of an understatement – it is radical (hence the name Radical Coaching), controversial and, some will claim, heretical!

It is not a book about coaching skills although it does include a few practical exercises where I've thought they might be useful. It's about the philosophy of coaching and about something not covered on most coaching courses: how to build your coaching business. Sandwiched between those parts of the book is a section about you, the coach: your motives, what success means to you and your ideal life.

This book is different for several reasons. Firstly, Radical Coaching is more than routine, run of the mill coaching; it is a breaking free from all the myths, fixed rules and techniques that surround coaching but that do not always deliver the results that clients are looking for.

Secondly, it is the result of over 35 years' experience as a coach. It's not a theoretical treatise. It's based on practical experience. Many chapters are therefore short, reflecting my musings and giving coaches food for thought.

Thirdly, it's a call for coaching to grow from its teen years into full adulthood, sweeping away much of the baggage that may have been useful in earlier times but that is now preventing it from coming into its full power.

Finally, it sweeps away a lot of the myths surrounding coaching in general and life-coaching in particular.

Few of the concepts in the book are original to me. Most of them were first suggested by someone else. The value of the book and of Radical Coaching comes from the synthesis and simplification of a lot of different ideas about coaching.

What makes Radical Coaching different is that it addresses the whole person. It rejects Descartes' delusion of any split between mind, body and spirit.

To put it another way, Radical Coaching is rooted in Spirit.

Before you worry that I'm going to get all religious on you, religion and spirituality are not the same thing. Spirit is not about dogma, ritual, philosophy or religious learning. It's not about "My beliefs are right, you are wrong!"

In Radical Coaching, Spirit refers to seeing the inner light in every person.

There is no 'one size fits all' option in Radical Coaching. The role of a coach is to see the oak tree in the client's acorn and, sometimes, to have more faith in our client's potential than they sometimes have in themselves. Most of all, Radical Coaching honors the Wisdom that created both the client's and the coach's Beings.

Simply put, the aim of Radical Coaching is to transform lives through hosting meaningful conversations.

This requires a fresh approach that revisits the roots of coaching.

Over the years, I have come to the conclusion that a lot of what is taught to coaches is wrong. A lot of false and misleading information has deceived coaches and their clients. This is what I want to sweep away. In doing so, I will be critically examining a lot of these most cherished coaching myths.

In case this sounds like the ranting of a deluded soul, the approach enshrined in Radical Coaching is based on life-affirming positive psychology. Many coaches, psychologists and psychotherapists have a profound understanding of how people survive in the face of huge challenges. Few of them can match that understanding with knowledge about what makes life worth living! Radical Coaching is a celebration of the miracles that lie waiting to happen in each person!

In this book I will be sharing some of the philosophies that have had the greatest impact on me, the origins of these approaches, how they work and their usefulness in Radical Coaching in helping coaches to host these meaningful conversations that transform lives.

I will show you the importance of the art of good conversations, using simple and easy to follow techniques that can be beneficial in your private as well as your professional life.

The conversation during the client's first session is vitally important in laying a strong foundation for future results. Coaches use the art of conversation to help clients create a clear vision of exactly what they want to achieve, the possible barriers that need to be addressed, the strengths to leverage and the opportunities to seize in order to inspire clients to 'go get' whatever lives they want to live.

We will be taking a detailed look at the key area of perception. An individual's perception is probably the most powerful tool in creating their reality. Most people do not realize the influence that their perception and their thoughts have on other aspects of their lives too.

As just one example, our thoughts trigger our emotions and determine the quality of our relationships.

Your perceptions are anchored in the world of thought. The key to controlling your reality is to learn how to control how you respond to your thoughts. In this book we look at different ways to leverage the power of thought.

However, it's not just our thoughts that influence our world. Positive emotions and a positive vocabulary have also proven greatly beneficial in improving peoples' general well-being and even their physical health. But your thoughts underpin both of these, which explains why Radical Coaching places so much emphasis on the way people think.

After exploring the different theories that can help a coach and client transform their client's reality, we will address how to build your coaching practice. One of the key tools I will take you through is the AIM strategy: Authority, Innovative offerings and Marketing. However, expect surprises!

But before moving on, who am I to be writing this book?

Who am I?

Mine is not a rag to riches story – I had a happy middleclass childhood with a good education. I got into the same scrapes most kids get into and came through them unscathed.

My first experience of anything traumatic came at 17 when, after a long battle with Hodgkin's' disease, my mother died. As well as being my mum, she was my confidante and best friend and it was a blow to my mind, body and spirit. The situation was exacerbated by my having to go into school and tell my brother that mum had died. I didn't handle it well and it wasn't until years later that I understood that there is no right or good way to break this kind of news.

A year later I left home to pursue a degree in physical education. Unfortunately, due to various communication issues within the institution, my tutors were not made aware of what had happened. I became increasingly depressed (although I did not know about depression then) and my behavior became increasingly erratic. Although I pulled through, thanks mainly to a friend, Gill Sasse, looking back on those years, they seem bleak.

Again, it wasn't until years later that my wife, Mathilda, helped me to understand that the end of a life is not the end of a relationship. The person lives on in your heart and in the memories you have stored.

As part of my teaching degree, I did my first coaching courses in 1977, in athletics and in field hockey.

Over the years, I have gained 6 sports coaching qualifications, each of which took at least a year to achieve. Contrast this with the weekend life-coaching courses that give participants certificates of competence!

In 1998, three things happened that have had a profound effect on my coaching: Firstly, I played hockey in goal for the England team that won the Over 40s World Cup. Quizzing the top coaches at a World Cup was a powerful learning experience. Secondly, I coached Somerset Under 21s to the County Championship title followed finally by being a part of the coaching team that led the West to winning the Divisional Championship. I learned a lot from coaching at the sharp end!

By the way, I don't believe that qualifications are essential for coaches, as long as coaches are committed to their lifelong learning. Being serious about coaching implies wanting to be the best we can be. This in turn requires that we are continually working on ourselves. I'm always confused by coaches who don't have coaches. What they are saying to the world is "I don't believe in the power of coaching!"

In 1986 I started working as a management trainer and coach in the UK Civil Service, where I began to learn how to transfer my sports coaching skills into the personal and business worlds. In 1990, I set up my own business and except for two 18 month periods, I have worked for myself ever since.

In recent years, I have become dismayed at how personal coaching (also known as life-coaching) and business coaching have become diluted versions of what they could be. Radical Coaching is my attempt to restore coaching to its full potential.

About 9 years ago, I completed both the NLP Practitioner and Master Practitioner courses and was fortunate to have done both under Richard Bandler, Paul McKenna and Michael Breen. It helped me to get NLP into context as their emphasis is on tools and techniques that work. They reject the flash techniques taught by so many NLP trainers.

NLP has gained a bad reputation in some quarters, mainly due to the outlandish claims made by many trainers and the development of techniques that only ever work in the training room.

Originally, however, NLP was a synthesis of many disciplines. NLP's detractors forget that the development of NLP came about from modeling the communication skills of Virginia Satir (a leading family therapist), Fritz Perls (founder of Ghestalt Therapy) and Milton Erickson (hypnotherapist par excellence).

NLP's founders, Richard Bandler and John Grinder added other material including "anchoring", the application of Pavlovian conditioning to people, and reframing, from Korbyski's mantra "The map is not the territory."

They also created the meta model of language, making clear distinctions between many different language patterns. Listening closely to the words your clients use will tell you a lot about them and for this, the meta model is a great tool.

Most important of all for me, I met my wife Mathilda on the NLP Master Practitioner course!

One of the questions I've asked myself over the years is why do we coach? What's at the root of our wanting to help others to help themselves? The problem with these questions is that they seem to lead to more questions, rather than to answers.

The closest I can get to an answer that works for me is contained in these wise words from Erich Fromm (1956): "The deepest need of man, then, is the need to overcome his separateness, to leave the prison of his aloneness."

Coaching, rooted in compassion, helps both the client and the coach to leave Fromm's prison. It helps us to melt away the gap between ourselves and others by enabling the coach and client to both be more human.

Notes:

Note 1: Some aspects of the concepts and some tools have been repeated. This was done deliberately, to embed them in your non-conscious mind more quickly!

Note 2: Most chapters are brief, reflecting my coaching thoughts and experiences. This also enables you to dip in and out of the book at will.

Note 3: The book has been divided into 3 parts:
- Part 1 deals with the philosophy behind Radical Coaching.
- Part 2 looks at you, the coach and hosting powerful coaching conversations.
- Part 3 addresses the issues surrounding building a coaching business.

Note 4: I have tried where possible to use the plural and "they", to avoid clumsy "he/she" or "her/his". Where I haven't, no gender stereotyping should be assumed from any use of singular personal pronouns!

:: PART 1 ::

CHAPTER 1: COACHING

"There are only two ways to live your life. One is as though nothing is a miracle. The other is as though everything is a miracle."
Albert Einstein

The History of Coaching

Coaching used to be reserved for the arts and sports worlds. Then, in the 1980s, Sir John Whitmore took the principles of sports coaching and introduced them into the business and personal worlds. In doing so, he introduced the GROW model much used by coaches and managers. I was fortunate in the early 1990s to attend a course run by Sir John, which introduced me to his work and to Timothy Gallwey's Inner Game approach.

Once coaching became mainstream, it rode the waves of therapy and specifically the non-directive counseling and psychotherapy approaches of people like Carl Rogers and George Egan. This meant that coaching adopted a non-directive, person-centered approach. In this approach, the coach's role is merely to create the conditions for change.

On the one hand, this enabled the coaching profession to grow very quickly but on the other hand, it left us with a very watered down version of what coaching could be.

Unfortunately, the situation has been exacerbated because this non-directive approach is endorsed by most of the professional bodies for coaching in their various skills and knowledge frameworks.

Radical Coaching recognizes that these person-centered, 'support but don't challenge' approaches to coaching, are not always appropriate and have their limitations. For example, non-directive coaching assumes that the client is the only person who should set the agenda for discussion.

This ignores the fact that many clients will avoid areas that are uncomfortable for them. Furthermore, non-directive coaches will often let their clients off the hook when the going gets tough for the client.

A further problem comes from confusion amongst potential clients. They are unsure about the differences between coaching, consulting, mentoring and counseling. In reality, these are four different approaches each with their own skill sets. However, they do all depend on effective listening and questioning skills.

In addition, the common ground in coaching and counseling is that they are both about the client, not about the coach/counselor. The miracles happen in the client – the impossible becomes possible in the client!

Unfortunately, in riding on the back of non-directive counseling, coaching has become a kind of 'therapy-lite' and has forgotten its roots, forgotten the skills of challenging and of confronting with tough feedback; and forgotten the opportunity for coaches to make suggestions when they know more about a particular situation than the client does or when the client has run out of ideas.

Theoretically, the ideal non-directive coach leaves no footprints in the sand, no indication of their presence. While many coach training organizations embrace this philosophy, once the new coaches go out into the real world, they soon discover that this is impossible.

Coaches bring prior knowledge, skills and experience to their role. If the client would benefit from hearing these, coaches cannot claim that they operate from the client's highest good while at the same time withholding their prior knowledge, skills and experience.

In addition, the more aware coaches soon realize that 'non-directive' coaching is impossible. The questions the coach chooses to ask, their body language, their tone of voice all mean that the coach cannot avoid being directive!

Radical Coaching insists that coaching has an important role to play alongside psychologists, psychotherapists, psychiatrists and counselors.

Until the 1940s, psychology had three purposes:

1. Unleashing potential.
2. Helping people to live more fulfilling lives and to feel a sense of purpose.
3. Cure mental dysfunction and illness.

Perhaps as a result of the trauma victims of the Second World War, from the middle of the last century, psychology focused almost exclusively on the third purpose, to the exclusion of the first two.

Indeed, until very recently with the advent of Positive Psychology, little empirical research had been carried out on the effectiveness of different approaches in achieving the first two purposes.

As you are about to discover, Radical Coaching is firmly rooted in Positive Psychology and some of its related approaches.

CHAPTER 2: TWELVE COACHING MYTHS

"I want to write books that unlock the traffic jam in everybody's head". John Updike

So, what are these coaching myths that are swept away by Radical Coaching?

Myth #1: Coach Training Companies (CTCs) are run by experienced coaches

Many people running CTC's are not coaches, or have only worked as a coach within a company and have never had to build a practice.

People think that the trainers on coaching courses are experienced coaches because many of the techniques taught on coaching courses make the instructors look superhuman! After all, the demonstrations always work, leaving the trainees really enthusiastic about applying these techniques in the "real world."

What you may not know is that the people chosen to be the "client" in these demonstrations were preselected. In other words there is nothing random about the choice.

One of the things that trainers are taught to do is to observe the audience and see who can access their feelings easily, who can visualize easily while in a conscious state, and who is very suggestible. With a "client" with those characteristics, no wonder the instructors look so good!

Myth #2: People are happy to pay a lot of money for coaching

This is bull****! I want you to engrave the following into your memory: **Clients don't pay for coaching; they pay for results!**

This is controversial, as a lot of coaches don't like being judged by the results they help their clients to get. Why not? Because they like to be able to blame the client for "failure", or justify it by saying things like: "The client wasn't ready to change." These coaches might like to ask themselves this: Would people such as Anthony Robbins, Rich Litvin, Daniel Wagner etc. be famous if they didn't get results?

The positive aspect of this is that if you are happy to be judged by the results you get, it will differentiate you from the ever-increasing number of life coaches being churned out by the CTC's.

Myth #3: Free taster sessions are great way of attracting clients

This is half a myth! (I may have invented a phrase here: 'half myth' sounds a bit like 'half pregnant' - it either is or isn't!)

I know that many coaches offer the first session for free as a way of demonstrating their ability as a coach. Under certain circumstances, it's a great way to start the relationship with a new client. But be careful! It all depends on how you do it because:

1. People don't value things that are free.

2. People have become accustomed to marketing based on 'free gifts'.

3. It seems inappropriate to offer for free something that is going to be life changing unless you position the free session correctly.

4. Coaches go about it in a wishy-washy way, being very vague about their purpose and then being defensive about fees. Often, the coach gets no commitment from the potential client, saying something vague like "let me send you an e-mail with the details and we can go from there." I know; I've done it!

5. It seems to me to be poor psychology. The client's mindset focuses on life coaching being a free service. You then have to switch their mindset to one where they have to pay.

A better way

Before I go any further, let me stress that this section describes just one option out of many. I will be contrasting two very different approaches in Part 3 of the book. One is exemplified by Steve Chandler and Rich Litvin's approach, the other by Christian Mickelsen's. Both have had tremendous success so remember, you always have a choice!

There is a much better way, one that not only overcomes the five points in the previous paragraph section, but is also sound marketing. Take a look at successful online coaches and marketers, specifically those that market with integrity and who are not part of the 'pile it high and sell it cheap' mentality.

Most of them build their whole business around the concept of a 'sales funnel'. Don't worry about the jargon! 'Sales funnel' is the term used to describe a marketing and sales structure that begins with offering potential clients a free product and continues with the client being offered products and services which become more expensive. You go from high volume, low cost products that many clients will buy to the other end of the funnel where you offer low volume, high cost solutions.

Incidentally, this is how a many of the successful coaches make a lot of money. They create a product that offers high quality, valuable content and give it away! This stimulates people's interest because they ask themselves: "If this is the quality of the free product what must the paid for products and services be like?"

Before the person knows it, they have bought an e-book for $29, a CD set for $99, and a few weeks later, in response to a telephone call or email, they buy into a coaching program worth thousands of dollars.

That initial freebie was the bait! The freebie doesn't need to be a written report, although with the free voice to text recognition software that is available, reports are easy to produce. You can record an MP3 and offer that; just make sure to buy a reasonable quality microphone! The built-in mike on your laptop or PC probably won't be good enough. To record and edit your MP3, Audacity is a wonderful piece of software, and it's free!

You can also create videos, which need not be more than a PowerPoint presentation with a voice-over narration.

Remember, a sales funnel isn't essential – you can be a very prosperous coach without one, as we will see in Part 3. However, it can help you get around a common problem: no matter how well paid you are as a coach, what happens if, temporarily, you can't coach due to illness, for example?

A sales funnel will provide you with passive income while you are recovering. However, it's your choice.

Whatever your choice of approach, as I have already mentioned, if you want to be successful as a coach, you need to master two completely different sets of skills: getting clients and then coaching them. Your coaching skills have to be top-notch and you also need to master business building skills. While many coaches panic at the idea of 'sales and marketing', it needn't be onerous.

One of the great things about being a coach is that if you do it right, establishing yourself as an expert coach, marketing yourself and coaching all overlap.

If you do want to start with a free coaching session, make it clear that its purpose is for you both to decide if you want to work together. Above all, don't short-change the potential client! My free sessions last about 2 hours and I won't end it until the client has experienced a major change and goes away energized and inspired.

If you do want to use free sessions, try the following framework, adapted from the coaches' coach, Chris Mickelsen:

1. **Step 1**. Help the client to get a crystal clear picture of what they want from life and which of the 8 pillars of personal success they wish to work on. These 8 pillars are, in no particular order, spiritual, physical, emotional, psychological, work, money, relationships, rest and recreation.

2. **Step 2**. Uncover the hidden challenges or competing internal programs that may be preventing the client from achieving the success they seek in the area identified in Step 1.

3. **Step 3**. Make sure the client leaves the session renewed, re-energized, and inspired to be successful in the area identified in Step 1.

The client is extremely unlikely to achieve what they want in one session – for example, if you are a health coach and your client wants to lose 20 pounds of body fat, they won't do it in one session.

Your job as a coach is to help them to understand Step 2 and also for them to leave believing in you and your ability to help them and believing they can achieve their goal.

Just remember, the major aim of this free session is for your potential client to trust you. I'll be suggesting other ways you can begin your free session in Part 3.

Myth #4: Coaching is an easy way to make money

80% of small business start-ups are not surviving and thriving within five years of setting up! Of the 20% that do survive those first five years, 80% won't last another five. In other words, only 4% are surviving and thriving after 10 years! If you want to be part of that 4%, it's obvious that you have to do something different from the other 96%.

Most of the 96% who failed had read the same books, attended the same workshops, been guided by the same 'experts' provided by training companies and professional bodies.

Of course, this is all information that most Coach Training Companies (CTCs) don't want you to know!

And to add insult to injury, many CTC's will go back to their newly-trained coaches, appearing to be sympathetic to the difficulties of building a coaching practice, and heavily market their "advanced coaching techniques workshop."

Myth #5: It's important to be able to work with anyone

When you are first establishing your practice, it is very tempting to work with anybody with a pulse and a credit card!

However, you will quickly find that there are some subjects and some kinds of people that you find more enjoyable to work with than others.

Life's too short to work with clients whose company you don't enjoy. They will quickly become your clients from hell! Being a successful personal coach depends on you feeling passionate about what you do and on the alignment of your passion, purpose and strengths.

No matter how much of a pain they are being, clients will soon notice when you are just going through the motions.

I quickly discovered as a sports coach that my real passion lies in working with people who are already good, and helping them to go to the next level – helping the best to become even better. On the basis that how you do something is how you do anything, I'm gradually moving my individual coaching to that market.

There is nothing wrong with referring a client who you don't enjoy working with to another practitioner. The most beautiful gardens all need regular pruning! And after all, one practitioner's client from hell is another practitioner's angel!

Myth #6: Coaching should be non-directive

For historical reasons, personal coaching (also known as life-coaching) is dominated by people who come from a non-directive counseling background. As soon as a coach challenges her/his client, these purists start tutting and becoming highly critical.

The way I look at it is this: the term 'coaching' was first used in sports and arts environments. I have coached winning teams at regional and national levels. I quickly learned that to be successful, I needed to strike the right balance between being supportive and being challenging. If a team or player is underperforming, the coach has to address the issue.

If the coach is only ever supportive, it creates a cozy environment reminiscent of a country club. "Coaching and Cappuccino" is the phrase I coined to describe this sort of 'support only' approach.

I'm not denying that sometimes you do have to focus on being 100% supportive. For example, if your client turns up for session and tells you that her/his parent has just died and they are very upset, then it is obviously your role to be supportive.

It's knowing when to be supportive, when to be challenging, when to be provocative. And all of this whilst remaining true to the maxim that you are dealing with the client's world, not yours.

It is all about appropriateness. On the opposite side of the coin, to the coach who only ever creates a cozy country club atmosphere, I was recently told of a coach who had heard about a mass murder of young children in a school. The coach wanted to know how to help the parents create a strategy for dealing with the situation! This isn't even a matter of good coaching, but one of common sense - people need time to grieve.

By the way, I am not suggesting that the coach should tell the client what to do. Any input from the coach should be no more than a suggestion and only after the client has exhausted her or his own options.

I suspect that the reason a lot of coaches do nothing more than listen empathically, paraphrase and ask the occasional question is because their training was brief. In the short time (sometimes as little as one weekend!) available on the course, this approach was the safest to teach.

I don't deny that this 'listen, paraphrase, ask' approach can be extremely powerful in some situations. Equally, there are times when more is needed.

I can already hear the sound of the cozy country club coaches' disapproval of this section! On the other hand, I don't mind as I object strongly to the dryness and lack of soul of much that passes for professionalism in coaching and in the psychology world.

Myth #7: The power of networking

There is some truth in believing in the effectiveness of networking. However, a lot of courses suggest that coaches must go to networking events. I've never found networking events to be useful. If they are run by professional bodies, these events usually end up being members all trying to sell to each other.

If they are run for the public, you can end up spending a whole day working on a stand for little return. The best you can hope for is to give away a lot of copies of your freebie and hope that people will come back to you in the future.

Where there *is* power in networking is in social media, as long as it is done properly. Too many people treat social media as an end in itself rather than as a means to an end. If you have set up a sales funnel, then the purpose of social media is to pull people to your website so that you can get them to sign up for your freebie and you can market to them from there.

I'm sometimes asked by coaches whether they should have a blog and my answer is: "If you want one and enjoy writing!" I enjoy writing, so I have a blog. It's not compulsory, it's a choice. Similarly, you don't have to use social media – it's not compulsory, it's a choice.

If you do use social media, use it to establish yourself as a credible authority figure in your field. It is easy to waste a lot of time on social media sites, so before visiting a site, before posting a comment, ask yourself: "Is this helping me to build my business?" Another question you can ask yourself is: "Am I adding value?" Best of all, perhaps, is to ask yourself: "Is this the highest and best use of my time right now?"

I know coaches who brag about the number of LinkedIn connections they have, the size of their Twitter stream, the number of Facebook friends they have and the number of "Likes" they have on their Facebook page. As far as I'm concerned, it's all irrelevant if it doesn't lead to people coming to your website and signing up for coaching with you.

Never underestimate the power of social media marketing. I have bought a number of courses from Rich Schefren, Lee McIntyre, Alex Jeffreys, (all three focus on building strong online businesses) Michael Neill, Steve Chandler, Rich Litvin, (all three are heavily influenced by the work of Sydney Banks, as am

I, and are great coaches), Daniel Wagner (leading expert on positioning yourself as an expert in your niche) and others.

I had never met any of them but bought their products and services based on social proof (other people's experiences and recommendations) and on the congruence of their marketing material. Yes I have made a number of mistakes, though not with the names mentioned in the previous paragraph (see bibliography at the end of the book).

For now, however, it is enough to recognize that you need to become a specialist if you want to be really successful.

Myth #8: Trust in the Law of Attraction

Many people have been seduced by the Law of Attraction and by The Secret. This seduction is based on a misunderstanding. It is a well-established tradition among spiritual, mystical and metaphysical teachers to give students part of the answer and leave them to figure out the rest for themselves. Rather than leaving their students to sink or swim, the teacher will often leave a clue in plain sight.

This is the case with the Law of Attraction and The Secret. In both cases, the part that was taught was the power of positive thinking to attract what you desire. This in itself was misinterpreted by some as the power of wishful thinking! The part that was left out with the importance of taking action, though the clue lies in the word "attraction". The formula is simple:

Success = Attract + Action.

While I do believe that energy flows were attention goes, (your thoughts determine the quality of your life) and you do need to focus on what you want and believe that you can get it, you also have to take action. The Law of Attraction and The Secret were never meant to be interpreted as meaning that you can sit on the sofa guzzling beer, think a few positive thoughts and receive your heart's desire!

After all, why would the Universe reward people who are unwilling to put in the effort required? Nobody is entitled to success, you have to put in the necessary effort and often, to persist through several failures. Just remember: failing is an important part of learning. Failing at something does not make you a failure.

Myth #9: I'm a great coach; I can do it on my own

Really? My business has really taken off in the last three years for one reason only: I have worked with a succession of mentors.

I see no point in reinventing the wheel. To me, it is simple: I can either waste years making the same mistakes that those who got to the top have made, or I can learn from them and speed up my journey. It took a while to recognize that my reluctance to be mentored boiled down to a matter of ego.

Mind you, I made some bad choices initially. Now I've struck the right balance for me. I am actively involved with several different mentors, each of whom helps in different ways.

In addition, I am a voracious reader and my Kindle is full of books from successful people in NLP, coaching, hypnosis, and building strong businesses. In that way I can keep up-to-date with current thinking."

There is another issue here – a coach without a coach is telling the world that he/she doesn't believe in the power of coaching!

I'm often told that one of my strengths is my ability to sift through what others have written and extract the gold from the rest of the pebbles and to then clarify and simplify. In the words of John Updike: "I want to write books that unlock the traffic jam in everybody's head."

Myth #10: The market is saturated

This is another one of those "half-truths"! Yes, there are a lot of coaches out there. However, the answer to this is the logical continuation of points 2 and 3 above.

The market is saturated by generalist coaches, coaches who will coach anyone on any topic. If you want to succeed, you need to identify your niche and build a reputation as an authority in that area (remember what was written above about social media marketing). There are a number of questions that you can ask yourself to help you to identify your niche and how to approach it. They will be covered in Chapters 22 and 23 of this book.

For now it is enough to recognize that you need to become a specialist if you want to be really successful.

Myth #11: All of the above is great but I just don't have the time!

There are two important business skills that you need to learn: the first is outsourcing; the second is automating. They are both about letting go – often, the only barrier to letting go of a lot of tasks is your ego! I know because it took me a long time to learn this particular lesson!

To start with automation, look at the key activities in your business, record them, and see if you can automate them. You'd be surprised at how many things you do that can be automated. Take this report as an example. I could have written it on a word processor, but I learnt a long time ago that my mouth works faster than my fingers! So I dictated much of the first draft using Dragon Dictate.

Outsourcing is all about finding other people to do tasks for you. You may be able to create a website but is it a good use of your time? You may be able to write articles for your blog but would it be more efficient to have them ghostwritten for you? I accept that outsourcing requires money and money may be tight when you first start out. However, it is one of these things you should do as soon as you can afford it.

Why are outsourcing and automating so important? Because they free you up to do the most important thing a coach should be doing: coaching!

I mentioned this earlier but it's worth repeating: a key question to always keep at the front of your mind is: **"What is the highest and best use of my time in this moment?"** Anything that drags you away from your highest and best use is a candidate either for automation or outsourcing, as fast as possible!

Myth #12: Coaching needs to become an accredited profession

This view seems to be gaining increased support. The argument goes that if coaching is to be taken seriously, it needs to become an accredited profession. On the surface, this seems to be a reasonable idea. On further examination, for several reasons, it is dangerous rubbish! Why?

Because it will reduce coaching to a mechanistic, one-size fits all discipline. It's easy to accredit people based on them being able to perform a set number of skills in a prescribed way to a high level of competence.

However, and it's a big however, being a great coach has nothing to do with the number of courses attended. You can learn all the coaching models and techniques you like and become a fine coaching technocrat. But great coaching goes much further and taps into the coach's intuition – and how do you accredit intuition? Some trainers of coaches disparage intuition as being too "woo woo". My question to them is, when you have a choice of 4 or 5 questions you could ask a client, all equally valid, what prompts you to ask one above all others?

Supporters of myth #12 point to the sports world where coaching is accredited by professional bodies. However, in order to coach soccer, for example, there are a range of defined skills and tactics that can be taught. The disciplines of personal and business coaching are far too wide for that.

The only way to do it would be for successful, highly skilled coaches to assess other coaches. And why would they want to? They're having way too much fun coaching!

CHAPTER 3: RADICAL COACHING

"Profound understanding requires paying attention to what lies behind the visible surface." Timothy Gallwey

As we've seen, Radical Coaching recognizes that the origins of coaching lie in the sports and arts worlds. In these environments, a coach has to balance being supportive with being challenging. As we've also seen, most coach training favors supporting clients rather than challenging them.

Challenge must be rooted in acting from the clients' highest good. Radical Coaches are always prepared to give feedback, to hold clients accountable; to take the client deeper than they have ever gone before. Only in this way can they host meaningful conversations that transform lives.

In order to host such conversations, a simple way to think about how to go about building a coach/client relationships is to think about CEST: **C**onnect – **E**ngage – **S**hare, going through these three stages again and again to build a relationship of **T**rust and mutual esteem that honors the wisdom that created both parties' Beings. This provides a strong foundation from which to stretch the clients thinking and challenge their perception.

This is also the purpose of the first free 2 hour session, (if you do them), in which you share a powerful coaching experience and then outline how you might work together.

The model breaks down as follows:

1. **Connect**. Make contact with the person you would like to speak with.

2. **Engage**. Get their permission to coach them so that they can experience a powerful coaching conversation that will transform their life.

3. **Share**. Share a powerful coaching conversation with them. As Rich Litvin is fond of saying: "Serve them so powerfully that they never forget their experience with you for the rest of their life."

4. **Trust**. If stage 3 was successful, they will now trust that you have the knowledge, skills and experience to be able to help them to achieve their goals.

5. **Outline**. Outline what working with you will mean, what your expectations are of them and what they can expect from you.

```
      Connect
  ↙           ↘
Outline      Engage
  ↑           ↓
  Trust  ←  Share
```

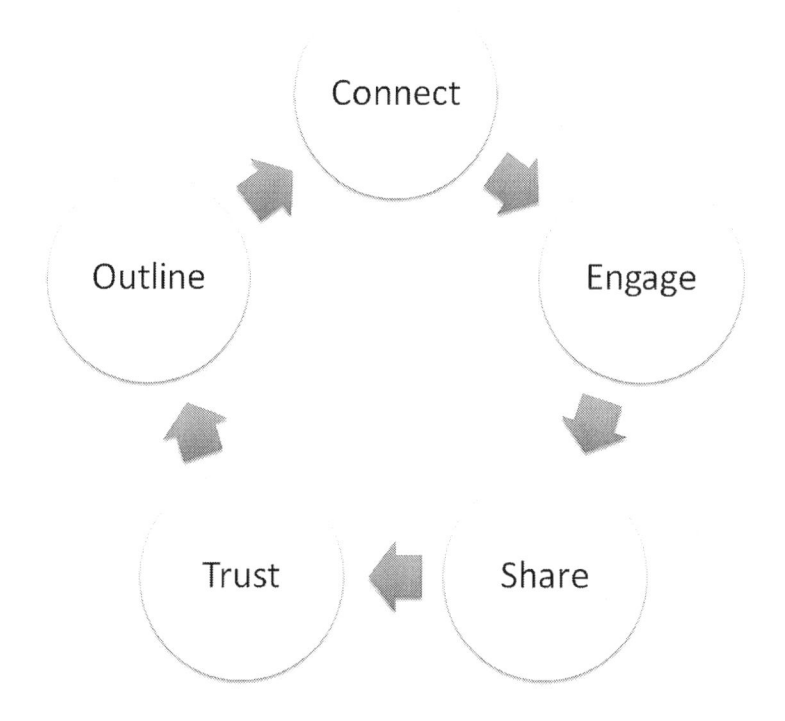

Avoid Collusion

To repeat something I mentioned earlier, coaches must avoid colluding with their clients' blame game and victim modes. Remember the cozy country club, "coaching and cappuccino" environment?

As a coach, you are not there to win a popularity contest or to be their friend. You are there to help them to achieve the results they are seeking. By the way, I've learned that the first goal the client voices is rarely the real goal.

To get around this, in response to whatever they say is their goal, ask: "What's important to you about that?" Keep on asking until their eyes light up and they speak with passion and/or conviction – then you know you've got to the real goal!

It's a sad fact that most coaches have a fear of demonstrating leadership that shows up as people pleasing and sycophancy. Perhaps the root of this is a desperate attempt to gain and retain clients! Whatever the reason, this explains why such coaches find it hard to retain clients!

Whether personal or business coaching, Radical Coaching rejects a 'one size fits all' approach, instead encouraging coaches to find their authentic voice and way to coach.

Radical Coaching is concerned with helping clients to challenge perceptions and beliefs, to examine their thinking habits, to overcome obstacles and in particular fear, all to achieve the results the client wants.

Radical Coaching recognizes that offering suggestions, advice and options is not the same as directing the client to a coach's pre-determined solution. Recognizing when a client may have run out of options and be stuck, a Radical Coach is happy to ask questions like: "Have you considered this option?" or "What would happen if...?"

I believe that if the coach has felt, thought, heard or observed something as a result of what the client did or said during the coaching session, it is unethical to hold back this information from the client.

Because clients pay for results rather than for coaching, it doesn't matter if a coach is directive or not as long as the client develops the right solution for them and is committed to it. And as long as the coach's advice is only heard once the client has run out of options.

Incidentally, I have never been challenged by a client about whether an approach is directive or non-directive. The only people that seem to worry about that are other coaches!

CHAPTER 4: RADICAL BUSINESS COACHING

"Only 4% of businesses are surviving and thriving after 10 years of existence. To be one of the 4%, you have to be prepared to go against the grain!" Nic Oliver

I'm only going to make a few observations about Radical Business Coaching in this book as I will be producing a complete course on the subject soon.

Radical Business Coaching rejects short term silo-thinking and pays attention to the wider context. It helps clients to think about their perception of their world and to reframe where appropriate.

Specifically, Radical Business Coaches look for a way to move the organization's mindset away from 'solving problems' that may or may not improve the situation. Instead, they focus on finding out what staff and other stakeholders want the organization to be.

RADICAL COACHING

A lot of conventional business coaching focuses on increasing the individual's skills without paying attention to the organization's needs. The focus is often on individual needs and not on improvement to the bottom line. This is what gives rise to the misconception that business coaching is a luxury.

Radical Business Coaches focus on balancing better business results with the client's individual agenda. This may involve discussions with the person being coached, their line management and the human resources department.

Radical Business Coaching also recognizes that many large organizations are unwilling to acknowledge the existence of the Elephant in the Room, let alone confront it. This is largely due to large organizations being both change resistant and conflict averse.

CHAPTER 5: THE RADICAL COACHING CONVERSATION

"Judgment comes from the intellect and brings negative feelings. Observation comes from wisdom and brings compassion."
Sydney Banks

Radical Coaching recognizes that there are three levels to a coaching conversation:

1. The relaxed discussion
2. The edgy discussion
3. The Core.

Non-directive coaching is ill-suited to helping clients to get to 'The Core'. By definition, in non-directive coaching, the client sets the direction for the coaching conversation. Most people are reluctant to enter Level 2, 'The Edgy Discussion', let alone Level 3, 'The Core', of their own volition. It usually requires the assistance of another person, in our case the coach, to move the client into those areas.

Incidentally, on another, related issue, one of the differences between therapy and Radical Coaching is that the latter assumes we are working with resourceful, performing people who can cope with and often relish being challenged and pushed. They want to be taken through the Edgy Discussion Zone level and confront the Core, the 'Elephant in the Room.'

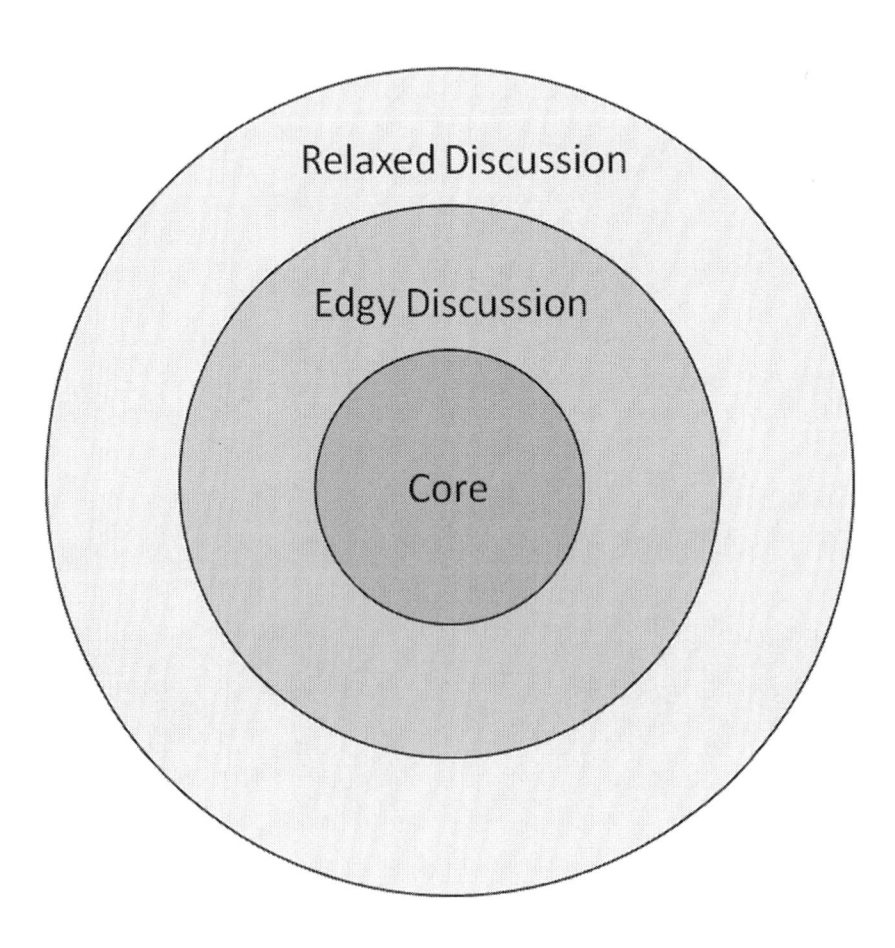

One of the things that differentiates Radical Coaching from many other contemporary approaches is the willingness to challenge the client, to not let them off the hook when they feel uncomfortable.

However, this is not an excuse for bullying the client. Done badly, confrontation is just as much of a mistake as is 'coaching and cappuccino!'

The key issue here is that challenging/confronting the client is not the same thing as telling them what to do. To clarify the differences, let's examine some typical examples:

1. **Telling:** "That won't allow you to achieve your goals!"

   Challenge: "Let's take stock for a moment. Will this decision help you to achieve your goals, or can you think of a better way?"

2. **Telling:** "You're only thinking of yourself – you don't seem concerned about other people's thoughts and feelings!"

   Challenge: "Imagine you were in a position of leadership – what would you do to ensure that you considered the needs of everyone involved?"

3. **Telling:** "You do know the answer; you're just avoiding the issue!"

   Challenge: "I know you say you don't know, but what might the answer be?"

4. **Telling:** "5 years is too long a timescale!"

   Challenge: "What if you decided to achieve your goal in 2 years instead of 5?"

5. **Telling:** "Your need for a better work-life balance will be compromised if you took that promotion!"

   Challenge: "I'm wondering how the value you place in work-life balance fits in with accepting promotion?

6. **Telling:** "You always seem to be blaming other people!"

   Challenge: "What part did you play in creating the situation?"

CHAPTER 6: RADICAL COACHING PREMISES

"We have the most wonderful job in the world. We find people in various stages of sleep. And then we get to tap them on the shoulder and be with them as they wake up to the full magnificence of life."
Sydney Banks, writing about coaching.

Let's list a few other premises of Radical Coaching. Radical Coaches:

- Are keenly curious, non-judgmental, quick to listen and seek clarification.

- Emphasize the positive.

- Value powerful positive questions.

- Focus on understanding and avoid judging and leaping to conclusions. In the words of Steven Covey, Radical Coaches "Seek first to understand, then to be understood."

- Speak their truth and face reality and coach their clients to do the same.

- Help their clients to face themselves. It helps people to confront any denial that exists.

- In businesses, help expose negative group thinking and organizational blind spots.

- Are prepared to give clients a compassionate kick up the backside if necessary.

- View people as miracles to be embraced, as mysteries to be explored.

- Specialize in the impossible, expecting miracles.

- Avoid a problem solving approach and focus on what is already working well for the individual. They help their clients to build on past and current successes. They focus on building exponentially on strengths rather than seeking incremental enhancements of weaknesses.

- Believe that people's thoughts define their reality and frames what they believe they can be. Radical Coaching is based on the principle that our feelings are triggered by our thoughts.

- Furthermore, all of our emotions that relate to the past are generated by our thoughts and perception. We are always free to reframe/rethink past unhappy experiences into interpretations that make us feel good.

- Believe that given a free choice, people will choose the option that makes them feel good. The fact that we often don't shows the existence of competing inner programs.

- Believe that people's mental, emotional and spiritual problems stem from faulty thinking. People are not broken, they don't need fixing; their thinking is faulty and needs reframing.

- Understand that the seeds of change are sown with the first questions that the coach asks. This is another reason why Radical Coaching considers non-directive coaching to be a myth.

- Recognize that language is full of metaphors and symbols and that we can learn a lot about a client's perception of the world from the metaphors and symbols they use.

- Help clients to establish a 'topic' for a coaching session rather than a 'goal'. Trying to achieve goals may lead to failure whereas a topic merely prescribes a something to explore.

- Help their clients to reframe the situation's content or context into something more positive when their clients are faced with situations they find challenging. (We usually overestimate the emotional consequence we imagine we will enjoy as a result of a decision we make. This is often the source of our unhappiness. For example "Once I buy that car/buy a new house/have a partner, I will be happy!" Once the car or house is bought or the person is in a relationship, they wonder why they still feel unhappy!)

- Are usually uninterested in the 'why' of a problem. Why is rooted in the past whereas people live in the present. Focusing on why can make us slaves of our past. Sometimes though, understanding why may help someone to better understand their problem. This is not the same as breaking undesirable thought patterns.

- Compliment and congratulate clients on what they are already doing well.

- Believe "If it works, use it. If it doesn't, do something else."

- Use scaling questions from NLP. "On a scale of 1 to 10 where 1 represents how badly you felt when we first met and 10 represents how you will feel when you no longer need to see me about this issue, how do you score yourself today?" They follow the client's response with a question like "What have you been doing that has raised your score from 1 to where it is today?"

CHAPTER 7: HARA POINT EXERCISE

"When adversity strikes, that's when you have to be the most calm. Take a step back, stay strong, stay grounded and press on." LL Cool J

You need two people to do this exercise. Doing it with a client will help them to understand the power of centering themselves.

This exercise is done with the client standing.

Push on the client's shoulder:

- Firstly side to side.

- Then backwards and forward.

Get the client to bring their focus into their Hara Point (on the center-line of the body, a palm's width below their navel).

- Get them to imagine breathing into their Hara Point.

- Get the client to connect with their inner power stored in the Hara Point.

- Push on the client's shoulder again (as above).
- The Client will now be a lot more centered and much harder to move.

Get the client to think of a fear/stressor/issue.

- Assess the intensity of the fear/stressor/issue on a scale from 1 – 10.

Push on the client's shoulder again (as above).

- The client will not be so centered and they should be able to feel how their body is reacting to the stress.

Get the client to clear their mind.

Get the client to bring their focus back into their Hara Point.

- Get them to breathe into their Hara Point and to connect with their inner power.
- Now think of the stressor again whilst keeping the focus in the Hara Point.
- The client should now be a lot more centered and much harder to move.

Assess the intensity of the fear/stressor/issue on a scale from 1 – 10.

You can also get the client to anchor this feeling of inner power and strength so that whenever they need it they just need to trigger their anchor.

This technique prevents being overwhelmed and makes people psychologically and energetically strong by tapping into the energy from the Hara, the biggest energy reservoir of the body.

Teach clients to use this technique any time they need to be in control of their state or need a confidence boost.

This is one of the most profound techniques for healing anxiety, panic attacks, phobias, low self-confidence, public speaking fears or stage fright. It is also a wonderful tool to give to children.

CHAPTER 8: SERVANT LEADERSHIP IN RADICAL COACHING

"How can I serve this client so powerfully that they never forget this experience for the rest of their life?" Rich Litvin

Serving clients is a core part of Radical Coaching, which is why Servant Leadership is important to Radical Coaches.

Robert K. Greenleaf was the first person to use the term "servant leadership", in an essay he published in 1970. In his essay he talked about the servant leader focusing more on serving those around him than on leading.

The aim of a servant leader is to help people and communities for the benefit of as many people as possible.

The world view around us is one that tends to want to lead instead of serve. Often the goal is to attain power or wealth and to control others. Not many people benefit from this type of leadership!

Even worse, so many leaders have a corrupt impression of leadership. Too many use their position of leadership to manipulate and even abuse their followers.

Others associate leadership with people at the top of organizations. If we accept that leadership is about making decisions about what is the right thing to do, we are all faced with leadership issues on a regular basis; and we are all leaders!

As a Radical Coach, or indeed any kind of coach, you must resist the temptation to take control or to take the power from your client. Instead do everything you can to place the power in your clients' hands. They need to shape their own path to the future.

Incidentally, it is not just an individual who can be a servant leader. Large organizations can choose to adopt this leadership style. This will be to the advantage of all its employees and consequently to its own advantage too.

After all, companies are made up of people. As a Radical Coach you can teach organizations how to apply this servant leadership model to their daily workings.

Below are 10 principles of servant leadership, identified by Greenleaf in his thesis:

1. Listening

In the ancient world, leaders were highly respected for their ability to communicate. These communication skills were crucial for good decision making. A Radical Coach will make it a high priority to understand the needs of his or her clients.

This understanding can only be achieved through the art of listening intently to what is being said and even to what is being withheld. Good listening skills require the combination of one's body, spirit and mind operating as one. This is needed to gather and process all the necessary information.

It also requires that coaches monitor their internal reactions to what they are hearing. Listening does not just involve relying on what the other person or group is saying. You should also rely on what your own inner voice is trying to tell you.

2. Compassion

Servant leaders not only strive to understand their clients, but also to 'feel' with them. Sharing similar experiences will help create empathy as well as showing your human side! By the way, never say "I understand how you feel" as we can never fully understand exactly what someone else is feeling!

Showing compassion will lead to feelings of acceptance and recognition of their uniqueness and inherent value. Radical Coaches strive to always suspect people of having good intentions even if their behavior suggest otherwise.

3. Healing

This is ultimately what brings about positive change in people and communities. Servant leaders however need to know how to become 'whole' themselves, before attempting to teach others do the same.

Greenleaf stated:

"There is something subtle communicated to one who is being served and led if, implicit in the compact between the servant-leader and led is the understanding that the search for wholeness is something that they have already."

4. Awareness

This refers to awareness in general and includes self-awareness. The aim of awareness is to support the servant leader in making discoveries needed to help other people. Sometimes these discoveries may be scary.

"Awareness is not a giver of solace - it's just the opposite. It disturbs. They are not seekers of solace. They have their own inner security." – Greenleaf

5. Persuasion

Instead of using authority and power, servant leaders rely on persuasion to guide the decision making process. This means that servant leaders should possess strong convincing and influencing skills that are completely deprived of force or coercion. This is the trick of getting someone to willingly join you in your corner, instead of forcing them into a corner.

A servant leader has a powerful ability to unite people.

6. Conceptualization

This is the servant leader's ability to 'dream big', usually against all odds. Radical Coaches see beyond the everyday reality to 'what could be' and not just 'what is'.

There always needs to be a balance between dreaming about the future and still staying in touch with the present. On occasion, Radical Coaches must dream big for their clients even when the latter are struggling to believe in themselves.

7. Foresight

This refers to a servant leader's ability to learn from the past, to accurately assess the realities of the present and to be able to predict the consequences of present decisions on the future. Radical Coaches help clients do the same.

8. Stewardship

Robert Greenleaf saw a future where every position in an organization, from the CEO to the tea lady, understood the roles they had to play. These roles would better not only their companies, but also the societies in which these companies exist. All of these individuals would be able to rely on each others' sense of responsibility.

In our context, a key part of Radical Coaching is helping clients to take responsibility for their lives and to see their role and their significant major purpose.

9. Commitment to People's Growth

Servant leaders are aware of each individual's inherent value, even if it not always visible. This knowledge is what motivates servant leaders to help others to unleash their potential and achieve optimum personal growth.

10. Community Building

Since small communities have been transformed into large institutions there has been a perceived "loss" of human power. Servant leaders are aware of these feelings. They strive to empower individuals to impact on change in their organizations and wider communities.

One way of achieving this is to facilitate unity among different people within the same organization or community. This is particularly important for Radical Business Coaching, where people often feel overwhelmed by their organization.

CHAPTER 9: COACHING FROM SPIRIT

"When I vowed to give up negative judgments of others as the foundation of my spiritual path, I quickly learned that this also meant giving up negative assumptions." Iris Barratt

More than ever, during these confusing chaotic times that we're going through, it's crucial that we can see gain and/or maintain some clarity through the deceptions that we're bombarded with. We need to be in touch with our Higher Selves and our Inner Wisdom if we are to thrive.

On the one hand, trying to define Spirit is like trying to pin down fog! The closest I can get is that spirituality is seeing the Inner Light in others. This Light encompasses the core values upon which all religions are built. If you look at these core values, you'll find:

1. Unconditional love for self, others and the Divine (however you define the Divine.)

2. Gratitude and reverence for our lives and for the planet.

3. The intent to set humanity free from delusions and illusions about themselves and about the world around us.

All else is a man-made construct to create religions. In many cases, the religion has moved away from the core values and focuses instead on dogma and behaviors that sustain the religion and its clergy.

I will be referring to Spirit but feel free to use whatever word (The Divine, God, The Universe etc.) works for you. For me, one of the purposes of the spiritual life is to set us free from our cravings for material things, for status, for power, for sex, for addictive substances and behaviors.

People look for guidance, 'the answers', meaning and the miraculous outside of themselves, never realizing that those answers lie on the inside. Spirit helps us to understand this and to see the nature of our existence and who we really are.

Of course, objects and behaviors will never satisfy these cravings. As soon as we secure one of them, fresh cravings arise. Radical Coaching can assist clients to break out of this vicious spiral by helping them to understand that the key question is not "What will satisfy me?" but rather "Why am I always unsatisfied?"

In case there is any confusion, the difference between religion and spirituality is that, unfortunately, religion has often been used in a way that tends to separate, exclude, condemn, criticize, punish, limit, cause friction and demand obedience. This is done without giving plausible explanations other than reciting verses from holy books that have questionable relevance to life today. Spirituality means harmony, peace, unity, freedom, spreading love, compassion, goodwill, joy and service to other people.

Religion is imposed by men who give themselves the power to rule over others, claiming it to be God's will and forcing people to give up their own God-given freedom of thought and will. Being in tune with the Spirit, on the other hand, makes you feel whole and protected.

I am not saying that Holy books are wrong, but you have to be smart to read through the pages to read the real true meaning of the messages.

It is essential to understand and to remember that all of life is spiritual. We are spiritual beings enjoying a physical life; we are not physical beings enjoying a spiritual life! Spirit, a Divine energy, penetrates everything that lives. Earth is spiritual, nature is spiritual, plants are spiritual, animals are spiritual and all humans both good and evil are spiritual. Spirit lives in each person, regardless of age, race, size, color sex etc.

There's a wonderful Hindu story that illustrates this:

A little fish swam to the Queen fish in her palace and asked her: "What is this sea I am always hearing about? Where is it?"

The Queen fish thought for a moment and then replied: "You eat, live, breathe, move, exist in the sea. The sea is inside you, outside of you, you are made of the sea and will live and die in the sea. The sea surrounds you as your own being."

In the same way, Spirit is an integral part of our being – we cannot be separated from it. At worse, we can only be unaware of its existence.

Spirit is still there, it does not care if you know it, recognize it or ignore it. Spirit just is. Where there is life there is Spirit.

Regrettably, that doesn't mean that everybody is aware of this fact or that everybody leads a spiritual life. Some people are more mindful and in touch with the Spirit within than other people. When you're aware, conscious of and in tune with the Spirit in everybody and everything, you're incapable of doing wrong or harm to anyone.

Why is that so? Because when you're in touch with Spirit, you know and are aware of the fact that you're connected with everything; that you are a part of the whole, and thus, if you harm others, you're harming yourself also.

Why are some people aware of what's out there while others are not? One simple reason is that there may be some obstacles that keep the person on a lower level of awareness of the expression of Spirit in their lives.

For example, a chronic negative attitude about life, a closed mind that refuses to learn and grow, pre-occupation with the daily mundane details and problems of the physical world, stress, anger, worry and tension, depression and fear, harboring resentments, envy, jealousy, revenge, or being too busy having fun like chasing money, sex, fun, power, alcohol or drugs. All these obstacles leave little or no room for your spirituality to find expression through you.

In light of the previous paragraph, it is clear that coaching in general and in our case, Radical Coaching is a Spiritual vocation. We help people to free themselves from the issues in that paragraph and most importantly, we honor the Inner Light inside each person.

Help your clients to feel safe and protected, free of fear and it naturally follows that they will grow in self-esteem. The more the Spirit within them is developed, the stronger these characteristics will be. Awakening the Spirit within doesn't happen through aggressive pursuit. We do not have to work hard on being spiritual; it's a state of being not of attaining. More than that, it's our natural state!

Remember, a show of genuine affection, a kind word, a phone call, a hug, a kiss, a little gift, or helping a needy person works wonders to make someone happy and to spread goodwill in our world. We all need to spread as much goodwill as possible around us to counteract all the misery in the world.

CHAPTER 10: PERCEPTION - THE POWER OF THOUGHT

"Consider the possibility that you may be far more able than you think and that when you let go of self-interference and increase your awareness, you will see exceptional ability emerge." Fred Shoemaker

What is Perception?

Perception is the way in which we perceive our world and the experiences we have of that world.

Radical Coaching acknowledges the power of perception in bettering the lives of individuals as well as helping businesses reach new heights.

Our perception is ultimately determined by our thinking processes. It was only a century or so ago that people first began to realize the importance of thought. "Thought" not only shapes our perception, but also our experience of reality. As a Radical Coach, you guide your client from a negative perception caused by negative thoughts to a positive perception driven by positive thoughts.

Just how important are thoughts in creating our perception? Let's put it simply: your thoughts and expectations about your performance determine your results!

What is Thought?

Two great questions for your clients: "Who would you be without your thoughts?" and "Who would you be without your fears?"

There are many possible answers to these questions but one thing will be certain. You are not the labels you or anyone else attached to you. You are the perfect you that you were born to be.

As a coach, your aim is to lead your client towards an understanding of exactly what "Thought" is. This has the potential to change the way in which they view problems as well as solutions.

The human mind consists of a conscious part and a non-conscious part (people often use the words subconscious or unconscious. I prefer non-conscious as subconscious implies under or inferior while unconscious has a connotation of being comatose!).

The conscious part can process as many as 40 bits of information per second. The real goldmine, in effective coaching, lies in your ability to help a client to connect with the non-conscious part of the mind. The non-conscious mind can process an incredible amount of up to 40 million bits of information in just one second. In order for an individual to control their thoughts they need to be able to connect with, program and reprogram their non-conscious mind.

More accurately, you can't control your thoughts, there are too many of them. What you can control is your reaction to your thoughts.

This theory also works the other way around. Radical Coaching aims to help a client access their non-conscious mind, in order to gain control over their thought life. The well-known example of an iceberg works well to demonstrate this. Just like an iceberg is made up out of the same water in which it floats, the mind is made up out of thoughts and this includes both the conscious and non-conscious mind.

Problems

A 'real' problem always leads to one of two options. You will either try to avoid dealing with the problem, or you will try and find a solution to the problem.

As a coach, you guide your clients to ask themselves whether the problem is indeed real. If it is a real, authentic problem, agree what they can do to either solve it, if a solution is available, or resolve to accept it as an unavoidable part of their life.

A question that Byron Katie uses is very useful here: "Do you absolutely know that this thought/perception/judgment is true?"

A Radical Coach will guide a client to become aware of the fact that perceived problems are also made up of thought.

Sometimes simply dealing with the thought can solve the problem.

This way an intimidating problem can sometimes fade back into the 'nothingness' where it came from, because it was only a thought and nothing more. Such a problem is usually not a real threat and sometimes just obscures an individual's view of new possibilities or even opportunities.

A Radical Coach knows that thought is the creator of all experiences, both good and bad. Consequently it may lead to the creation of both problems and opportunities. As human beings, our potential for new thoughts and ideas are off the map – they are endless!

This means that an unhappy person can change in an instant into a fulfilled individual, like a green plant sprouting up through concrete rubble cracks. If this plant is nurtured it can anchor its roots and experience life at levels never seen before. Each person is always just one thought away from either a happy, fulfilled life, or an unhappy, 'wasted' life.

You may ask: "What should I tell my clients to do in order to achieve this?" The answer may surprise you: "Nothing". It is usually only when we surrender all control over the outcome, that we find the pieces of the puzzle falling into place, usually revealing the image of a life only dreamed off; a life filled with a rewarding career, compassionate relationships, selfless wealth and unimaginable happiness.

Thought and Happiness

One of the main reasons why people turn to coaches is because they find themselves lacking joy and contentment in their lives. It is often not the poor or the uneducated that seek help from coaches. Instead it is often the rich and successful who are still searching for inner peace or happiness. Or, they have discovered that what got them to their current level of success is preventing them from moving to the next level.

As we now know, happiness is an inside job and once again, the creator is thought. Radical Coaches know that feeling empowered or disempowered has more to do with our own inner perception than with the actual outside world.

In this case it has to do with how we perceive ourselves while we are living in this world. We can either see ourselves as being victims of our world or rulers over it. Once again, this negative or positive perception is determined by our thoughts.

If you are still unsure about what I am talking about, consider something we have all experienced before: a bad day... Even Radical Coaches will sometimes experience a bad day - we are only human, after all! Can you remember the last bad day you had?

Usually on a bad day it feels like everything just goes wrong. It feels like almost everybody you know, and even don't know, woke up that morning with the common goal of seeing just how far you can be pushed. Sounds exaggerated doesn't it? And it is.

You see, the day itself is 100% neutral. The day itself is neither good or bad, it is what it is. However, you have the power to perceive it as being either good or bad. This perception is based on your thoughts. Moods are nothing but an inexplicable change in thoughts. This brings us to our next point.

Thought and Emotions

As a Radical Coach, it is crucial that you help your clients to understand that even their emotions are controlled by their thinking patterns. How a person thinks will influence how a person feels.

As mentioned in the previous section, moods are just reflections of fluctuations in a person's way of thinking. The reason why our thoughts can change so rapidly is still unclear. It is however accepted that a change in the *quality* of thoughts ultimately gives rise to a mood.

As a coach you can help your client control their moods. You should alert them to the fact that their moods are caused by nothing more than just plain, simple changes in their thinking. We as human beings are not helpless victims of our 'temperaments'.

We can decide how things should be - we are the creators of our world.

I hope it's clear to you that emotions and thoughts do not exist as completely separate entities. The one influences the other (more on this in the following chapters and in particular, Chapter 13.) Thought is the causative agent, while emotion is what happens as a result of the thought. A Radical Coach can help people understand this and apply it to their everyday life.

Thought and Relationships

How we act in a relationship and even the priority we assign to one relationship over another is greatly influenced by how we perceive or think about a person. Our thoughts on that person will influence our opinion far more than the individual's actual characteristics. This implies that we run the risk of thinking 'falsely' about a certain person.

"You are not the man/woman I married anymore." This is a line we have all heard before, whether in real life or only in a movie. The right question to ask in response to this remark would be whether you really ever knew the person as they truly are or as you would have wanted them to be?

The statement at the beginning of the last paragraph may also be an indication that during the courtship phase, the other person disguised or hid their true nature. If you are coaching the 'hider', challenge them on why they felt the need to hide their true selves. Ask them to think of times when people did react positively to their true rather than disguised self.

If you are coaching their partner, ask them whether they have been misled by others in the past and see if a pattern emerges.

When you are coaching clients who are struggling with their marriage, you may need to draw their attention to the fact that they might have created a person in their mind who never really existed in the first place and who was never the person they chose to marry.

A Radical Coach values the treasure in every person, however deeply buried it may be! The coach's task is to recognize the treasure within, treasure that in most cases is waiting to be liberated, awakened, empowered, energized and used.

The danger of your clients having the wrong perception about their spouse/child/sibling is that they might miss out on the real 'magic' inside of them. They have created a false counterfeit image that has no substance to it. The good news is that as a coach, you can 'introduce' them to the real person. This can only be done once they are willing to acknowledge their part in thinking the wrong way about the individual.

Our Perception of Time

Most of us operate under the illusion of time. In fact, what we are doing is worrying about things in the future, which are not yet a reality. We have no influence over these things yet. The other side is regretting things of the past, which are dead and gone and can't influence us physically anymore.

Radical Coaching recognizes the role our thoughts play in our, often wrong, perception of time.

Life is lived in the moment and there will never be another day like today or another hour like this one. So why do clients waste it worrying about things that may never happen or regretting things that can't harm them anymore?

The 'past' is nothing but memories and memories are nothing but stored thoughts. The 'future' is our hopes and dreams, but these are still only thoughts. Neither one is in fact 'real', unless we unwisely choose them to be.

Radical Coaching involves freeing people's minds from illusory realities and bringing them back into the present.

Thought plays such an important part in the creation of our life experiences that a theory exists to explain both the importance of thought, and the link between thought, consciousness and mind. The Three Principles Theory (see Chapter 13) exists to help people change their thoughts. Its aim is to shift their focus from what they do *not* want in life to what they actually *do* want.

The practice of the Three Principles can motivate an individual to reach a much better quality of life than they could ever have imagined.

Two other psychological theories which closely resemble the Three Principles approach are those of Positive Psychology (Chapter 15) and Appreciative Inquiry (Chapter 20). The main difference is that the latter two concentrate on the power of words and actions, instead of thought.

CHAPTER 11: REFRAMING YOUR PERCEPTION

"Humans see what they want to see." Rick Riordan

This chapter is just as relevant to coaches as it is to clients. Without some personal experience you may come across as not knowing what you are talking about.

Rookie coaches usually have a bag full of techniques and do not always know when to apply which technique where. The 'Paralysis by Analysis' phenomenon may keep them focused on choosing the 'perfect' option for so long that their clients may become demotivated and loose interest in coaching altogether.

Other new coaches (and some not so new coaches) wander around with a bag full of 'solutions', looking for a problem that fits!

Weirdly, when I did the NLP practitioner and Master Practitioner courses, my mind lingered on very few of the techniques. One of those was reframing.

Reframing Categories

As human beings we like to put things in boxes, we like to categorize people, events, circumstances, etc.

The problem is that these 'boxes' do not stand alone, but can actually influence one another. Often, one 'bad' box has the ability to interfere with our enjoyment of all the other many 'good' boxes; like the one rotten apple spoiling the whole harvest. This one bad apple can almost completely distract our attention away from all of the good things we have to be grateful for in life.

Incidentally, it's a characteristic of depressives that they have an inability to remember the good boxes; they only remember the bad ones!

We all have an opinion on what we consider to be fair in life, but what is fair? Fair is nothing else but a category we have created.

For example, imagine that a friend at work gets promoted over you. You may feel it is not fair because you have been working there for longer or you have been working harder. Let us flip the coin to the other side. What is the lesson for you? What do you need to change so that next time, you get promoted?

Similarly, the beggar you pass on the street may feel that is not fair that you get to drive a fancy car or sleep in a fancy house, just because your parents had enough money to send you to a good school and college afterwards.

Perhaps the beggar was obliged to leave school early to earn an income to help support sick parents. Now, in the recession, with a scarcity of work, the beggar believes that the only option is to beg for money. Is that fair, because you are on the 'good' side and the beggar is on the 'bad' side? What is fair? It is just a category.

So what if your friend got that promotion over you? You are still healthy; you still have a good marriage and a nice house, a good income and food on the table.

Reframing Stress

Often, the secret to success is not the ability to ignore stress, but rather to 'reframe' that stress. The most successful people in life view stress as an essential part to achieving success. Many underachievers view stress as an obstacle in their road to success.

In coaching and playing sport up to international level, I've seen over and over again that a difference between those who succeed and those who don't, even when better skilled, is the ability to reframe stress. Specifically, the ability to see stress as an enabler, rather than disabler of performance.

In the next section, we will look at perception as shaping your reality. If you want to change your reality change your perception first. Reframing is exactly that: changing your perception. Your 'frame' is nothing else but your reality. The formula is straightforward: Perception = frame = reality.

The secret to using stress in a productive way is to 'reframe' your perception of it, from being an unwanted obstacle to a welcome 'motivator', necessary for success. This way you will see a new situation as an exciting opportunity, instead of an impossible task.

History is full of people who suffered horrifying ordeals and then later refer back to those troubled times with gratitude and not bitterness. It is very seldom that a certain event can be seen as being just 100% bad.

In the end, words like 'good' and 'bad' are just oversimplifications. They do not take into account the whole spectrum of possibilities that may have emerged from certain circumstances. If you want a powerful example of this, read Victor Frankl's book (2004).

Perception and Reality

Just like a priest, a police officer and a successful business man will naturally view our imaginary beggar in different ways, so too our perception will influence how we see and experience the world around us.

Each one will put the beggar in a different frame and consequently experience different emotions towards the beggar. These emotions will flow over to their actions and determine whether they will respond neutrally, positively or negatively towards the beggar.

This is just a simple way of demonstrating how our thoughts can influence our emotions, actions and consequently our reality. Reframing, or changing your perception is key in changing your reality.

A great example of reframing perception and reality happened when my wife's nephew was 3 and his grandfather, my father-in-law, had his 70th birthday. My father-in-law was saying that it was no fun getting old; his grandson, Shade, was saying:

"Grandpa, you should be pleased that you're old."

"It's no fun being old" his grandpa replied; "your bones ache, your hair falls out..."

Shade climbed up onto his grandfather's lap so that they were sitting nose-to-nose and he said firmly: "Grandpa, you should be pleased that you're old. We're pleased that you're old, because if you weren't old, you'd be dead!"

Get to the Core

Successful coaches know how powerful their clients' perceptions are. In your coaching conversations, your intention is to get to the heart, or the core, of their being, their perceptions which determines their reality and not waste too much time talking about more superficial things.

Keeping on asking "What's important to you about that?" will help you get to the core and unearth things the client may not even be aware of!

Even when people approach you for coaching, understand that during your first session, you are still a stranger to them. Initially, the chances are that they will not naturally open up their hearts towards you. They will still feel vulnerable and only share superficial bits and pieces about themselves. In the end these will not be very useful in achieving the required results.

In simple terms, this means that what they may present to you as their first 'goal' won't be their real goal, since they are not comfortable to let you in yet. These are frames that they have created and may only influence them in a negative way. In one of the following chapters we will be taking an in-depth look at these self-limiting frames.

Of course, the good news you can share with your clients is this: just like you can change the frame of a picture, they too can change these frames that keep them trapped in a world they don't want to be in.

At this point a note of warning is probably appropriate: never underestimate the power of an old frame, or how hard it may be for some people to recognize these old frames!

Remember that our perceptions shape our realities and if they perceive this old frame as an objective truth (a real unchangeable thing) it may present somewhat of a challenge. When you confront people with the concept that there is no such thing as objective truth, it may cause them to feel insecure and out of control.

Oddly enough, what it does is it puts the control right back into their own hands, which is the exact opposite of what they experience emotionally.

Ownership

To be able to change something, anything, we need to take ownership of both the original situation and of the changes we make. These self-limiting frames are no exception.

It is quite sad to realize how many people have 'adopted' the frames of others, instead of creating their own frames. As children we are constantly exposed to 'fixed' or 'objective' frames and taught to rely on these. As we grow older we become more and more aware of the frames created by society of what is acceptable or not.

This is not always a bad thing. Often, other people's frames may indeed be useful and beneficial to you too. Accepting a frame just for the sake of pleasing others, however, is never a healthy exercise.

As a coach you can help your clients open their eyes. They may just see, for the first time, that 'truths carved in stone' may in fact be only small clouds, easily blown away by a simple change in perception. This is called reframing. By applying the correct, powerful frame to each situation in their lives they may free their potential and become all they can be.

You may wonder how you can practically help your clients reframe their perception. Let us first look at how you can't do it.

Remember that you are the coach and that the power is always in your clients' hands. You can help them understand that they have the power and all the wisdom and ability to use this power to stay in control regardless of the ever-changing circumstances around them.

So it is not by taking control out of their hands. Instead it is through helping them understand that they are already, and have always been, in control.

Often this first 'goal' or first 'question' is still just a superficial sharing, instead of core issues. As a coach you should not be blinded by this superficial first 'goal', but instead try and get to the core of what lies beneath this superficial issue. "What's important to you about that?"

Once you get to the core, don't be surprised to find some self-limiting beliefs. These are nothing but people's perceptions, or frames, about themselves or their circumstances that prevent them from reaching their full potential.

A great part of your role as a Radical Coach is to help people recognize these self-limiting frames, which often form part of a weak self-image.

Secondly it is not about them controlling their thoughts either. If you have ever tried controlling your thoughts you probably would have found it to be an impossible and very frustrating task. There are just too many of them! Instead it's about your clients controlling how they respond to these thoughts.

Now that we have looked at the 'don'ts' of reframing let us look at the 'dos'. At this stage, I should point out that these techniques should be used in an ethical way, to benefit your client and not misused manipulatively.

Reframing Techniques

1. Metaphor

We all use language in our daily communications with each other. Often we use metaphors without even realizing it. For instance, have you ever been 'stuck' in traffic? It is a metaphor, because you were able to get out of it, even just by getting out of your car and walking around the block.

Metaphors are just oversimplifications, and these are seldom true. As a coach you can focus your clients' attention on those metaphors that may be distorting their view of reality. Once they notice them, it may free their perception and make it more pliable to change.

People often don't realize the power of words, and especially metaphors, in creating their reality.

2. Rapid Change/Disassociation

When you are too close to a certain situation, it may be difficult to see all aspects of it. The best way to get a better view is to take a step, or if needed a few steps back. This way you can see all the way to the borders of the problem. You might even realize that it is not as big as you initially thought.

This process of putting a distance between you and a situation is called disassociation. It is only logical that the further you step back or disassociate yourself from a problem, the smaller it will appear and the more of it you will be able to see. You might even see how better to deal with the situation, a possibility that wasn't visible before because you were standing too close.

Disassociation may also be termed the 'helicopter view' in which you literally hover above a situation and look at it from a different perspective.

A great way of doing this, which Anita Sheehan reminded me of recently, is to ask the client what they would do if they were in the other person's shoes or what they would suggest if they were the coach and you were their client.

Disassociation is a very powerful tool to immediately lift a burden from a client's shoulders. It can change their entire perception and consequently their reality in an instant. It can open their minds to new opportunities and new solutions they haven't considered before.

As I am sure you can see, disassociation is a very powerful tool. It has the potential to bring about immediate change in people's perceptions, reality and emotions.

3. Rainbow Mindset

Just like a rainbow consists of a variety of colors, life also has colors to it; it is not just always black and white. Many people have an 'either-or' perception. Something is either seen as being black or white; right or wrong.

The truth is that the exact same events can be categorized as being both good and bad. Think about a sports event for instance. There will always be a winner and a loser. The winner will of course see it as being a good event, while the loser will see it as a bad event. In the end it still remains the exact same event.

As a coach, you guide your client to notice the full range of colors or at least the different shades of grey.

Now these three tools of reframing can be used to help your clients, but furthermore you can also apply them to yourself. They will assist you in becoming free from unhelpful frames and to unleash your full potential as a great Radical Coach.

It may take some time and effort to learn how to use these skills and techniques. The results will however be worthwhile, and that is after all what you and your clients are after-results.

Advanced Reframing

There are two words that will almost always be a part of learning any new skill and these two words are 'confusion' and 'contradiction'.

Confusion is often seen as being a bad thing, but in fact confusion often leads to learning. It is the motivation behind the whole process of wanting to find new information and for studying it in the first place.

Contradiction is due to one of two things: it can be a symptom of simplifications which are incompatible with each other. This is often a result of seeing the world as black or white, instead of acknowledging the full spectrum of colors and shades in between. Alternatively, it can be a sign of competing, mutually exclusive, internal programs.

Coaches need to feel comfortable with confusion and contradiction and recognize that these two are two normal aspects of learning and are part of any client's path to the discovery and reframing of their perceptions. It may be easy to become distracted by all the confusion and contradictions that a client may suddenly need to face. Remember that in the end it is the results that are important and not the process of getting to the results.

When confusion and contradictions cause a client to become distracted or demotivated, you can help guide them along by using the following three steps.

Remind them that their reality is created by their perceptions and in order to change their reality they need to change their perceptions or frames first. Then help them do the following:

1. Ask themselves whether their current frames are useful and positively influencing their lives.

2. If the answer is 'no', help them decide on a better frame to replace the old one. This frame needs to be supported by positive input.

3. Once this new frame is in place, help your client to avoid depending on others to accept, approve or validate the new frame. Frames should stand alone, independent from other people or circumstances. It is the client's mind, their life and their reality, nobody else's.

The most powerful frames will ultimately determine the client's reality, so help them enforce those frames that will benefit them most in the end.

CHAPTER 12: SELF LIMITING FRAMES

"The power of our beliefs can work in either direction, to become life affirming or life denying." Gregg Braden.

As a Radical Coach, you need to be aware of the faulty compromises you have made with regard to your perception. So in this chapter we are going to shine the spotlight on you and not your clients. If you understand some aspects of how your mind works, you will better understand how your clients' minds work.

"Healer heal thyself" is a well-known saying which indicates that by being able to heal yourself you will better understand the healing process. You will be able to empathize with your client and guide them every step of the way, because you went there first.

Of course you first need to understand the theory behind reframing your perception and this is what this chapter is all about. It will help you to 'see' the wrong frames and perceptions that are keeping you captive.

It will help you to break free from these frames; you will know it is possible; it can be done and it will add to your confidence in helping your clients do the same.

To recap: as human beings our realities are created by our own biased perceptions. In this context, 'biased' means that we decide what is important and what is not; what is good and what is bad. We choose how our frame of reference must look, what it should include and exclude and what is good and bad within this frame. This is a natural process that most people are not even aware of.

There is no way of proving that one frame of reference, or one perception, is better than another. Remember Byron Katie's question? ("Do you absolutely know that this perception/
thought/judgment is true?"). So how do you judge your frame? Isn't the best way to determine which frame will ultimately benefit you the most and then choose to see life through that perspective?

This may sound easy, but as I mentioned before, controlling your thoughts is not possible. There are too many of them! What is far easier than controlling your thoughts is to control how you react to them.

We will all be confronted with negative frames, either from ourselves or from other people; it is unavoidable. How you react to those negative frames is what is important.

For example, let us take a young boy who believes that his brother is smarter than he is. Where did he get this frame? Perhaps from a teacher or from mishearing his parents in conversation. The boy can react in one of two ways to this negative frame.

He can either use it as an excuse to do as little studying as possible, or he can see it as motivation to work harder at school and prove the teacher and his parents wrong. The important question is: What frame will most benefit the boy over the long term?

What you believe to be true will ultimately become the frame you choose to live in. The important thing is: this frame will create a corresponding reality. It will affect your behavior and the choices you make to give life to this frame; to make it real.

As with all things in life, there are exceptions. For instance: The law of gravity is real. If someone says you can't fly and you decide that you will not accept this 'negative' frame and jump off the nearest building, you will end up with at least a few broken bones. The important question remains: "Is this frame beneficial to me or not?"

We all have a 'realist' within ourselves. It is the subtle voice of your conscious mind asking "How do you know this will work?" "What if you fail?" "Where is the proof?" If you think about it, you will realize that most of the proof we have in this world originated from someone's actions. Their actions were rooted in their perceptions about what could be and not in what already is. Eventually this gave them the proof they were looking for.

So once again a better question would be: "How can this perception (and the consequential actions and realities) be useful in some way?" The wrong question is: "Is it true?" Truth is not always an objective reality and it is usually determined by your perception. If you can change your perception then you can change what is true or 'real' about your life.

To change your reality start with changing your perception, but it does not end there. Our perceptions influence our actions and it is ultimately actions that bring about change. Your frame, or perception, needs to be so strong that it will ultimately affect the way you do things.

How do you strengthen your perception to the point where your actions naturally become affected by it? Firstly, be aware that you may need to silence the negative inner voice telling you that it can't be done. You can refuse to accept a negative frame from the outside and you can reject a negative frame coming from within yourself.

Secondly ask the most important question: "Can this new frame benefit me in any way?" It is as simple as that. Then back-chat that negative inner voice with confirming statements like: "Of course I can do this." "It is not as hard as it looks."

Remember this is only the beginning! First, change your perception. Secondly make sure that this new perception influences your actions. Sometimes, performing certain actions can actually help to strengthen your perception. It has the added benefit that future actions may become easier as your new frame is encouraged.

If you can just manage the above steps, many of your self-limiting beliefs will be a thing of the past. You will be more in control of your own life and on your way to fulfilling your dreams.

Let us take a last look at the three most important questions to vanquish any self-limiting frames:

1. "Can this frame benefit me in any way?"
2. "What is the best frame for me in this specific situation?"
3. "What actions can I perform to strengthen this frame and make it real?"

Most of us already have everything we need to be successful. What proof do I have of that? Well, no proof, but the frame is beneficial and I decided that I would accept it as true and real. It's a useful frame for me as it influences the way I treat people. Consequently they have become exactly the way I perceive them to be. In this way, my frame is also helpful to other people.

These three questions won't only change your own self-limiting frames, but also the self-limiting frames of others. It can replace something negative with something positive. It can turn a lifeless frame into a constantly creative and productive frame. It can guide your actions to improve your own life as well as the lives of others.

So, regardless of who you are or where you find yourself right now, think of some of the self-limiting frames you have compromised on. In other words, think of anything that you believe you can't do.

Maybe you can't think of a self-limiting frame right now, but perhaps later you will spot one in the way you talk about yourself or the actions you choose to avoid. What is important though is that you realize that you have control over these self-limiting frames and that you can change them.

The above information really holds the key to changing your perceptions and ultimately turning your life around.

Next, we will look at the two most popular self-limiting frames that most people in the Western World aren't even aware of. These two frames are so powerful that they stand between most people and success.

The first one is the self-limiting frame of scarcity. Consider the following statements:

- "I don't have enough time."

- "I don't have the money to..."

- "Why did this happen to me?" or "why is this happening to me again?"

Do any of these sound familiar? Are any of these statements based on fact, or are they just the opposite of an abundance mind frame? Let us look at it in another way. Are you reading this book on a computer? Did you purchase this book with money you owned? Do you actually have time to read this book?

If you answered yes to the above questions the truth is that you are not that badly off after all. You have enough money to own a computer, to buy the books you want and you have the time to read them.

So what if your new sports car is not paid off yet and you need to work an extra ten hours a week to pay all your bills. Do you really need a sports car to start with? It was your choice to buy it, so it's up to you to do what you need to do to pay for it! Are you healthy? Did you have a nice supper last night? All your physical needs are fulfilled. You are OK.

Take a look around you. There is not really a scarcity of anything in the world. There is even enough food in the world, it is just poorly distributed so that some people have more and others have less. There are other things that have value besides just food.

All people are in some sort of relationship. How many friends do you still have from 20 years ago? Did you make some new friends over the past 20 years? See, there are enough people in the world to be friends with and to have a relationship with. If you dump this boyfriend, who might be treating you badly – he is not the only man in the world! You will find someone new.

A big mistake to make at this stage is to confuse a 'carefree' life with a 'careless' life. You can't go around treating people badly just because you think there will always be someone else waiting around the corner. You still have a responsibility towards yourself to become the best you can be. So work when you need to work, treat people with courtesy, but don't live in panic because of a scarcity mind frame.

The opposite of scarcity is abundance. Can an abundance mind frame be more helpful than a scarcity mind frame? It might motivate you to pay for that course you always wanted to do, but always thought you couldn't afford. In turn it can help you to progress at work or even open up a new, more fulfilling career altogether.

You may wonder what is really so bad about a scarcity mind frame that will make all the effort worthwhile. Have you ever been cheated in a business deal? The reason behind that is a scarcity mind frame. Do you get frustrated when standing in a long queue for a long time? That is because of a scarcity mind frame.

Can you see how the scarcity mind frame has infiltrated our thought world? It's even one of the reasons we become rude towards other people!

The truth is that there is more than enough in this world for everyone. There is enough time; there is enough money to afford the basic needs of life. If you understand this, it will take a large load from your shoulders and you can help others do the same too.

Let us consider another more common indicator of the scarcity mind set: jealousy.

We all know at least one person who has something we want, but cannot get. It can be something as simple as a nice figure, a beautiful face; maybe something more important like a promotion at work or wealth.

It is possible that the person is your friend and secretly you feel bad about being jealous, because they really deserved success in some way or another.

Don't beat yourself up. You are human after all and that means that you are not perfect. Guess what: your friend isn't perfect either, despite her success. Accept the self-limiting scarcity belief.

In one sense our self-limiting beliefs offer us protection, so it may have served you well until now. Sometimes we have to understand that a self-limiting belief has reached its "best by" date and simply replace it with a more useful frame of mind.

The next self-limiting frame is that of resistance vs. acceptance. We are all sometimes faced with a daunting task like leading a meeting or giving a speech at a seminar or conference. Usually the first idea that comes up is: "I can't do this."

Now there are only two ways in which you can respond to this negative self-limiting frame. The first is that you accept it as being true and you try to find a way out; 'play sick so that you don't have to go to school' kind of thing. The problem is that it may indeed be good for you (and for your future promotion prospects) to lead a meeting or give a speech. You deprive yourself because you accepted a negative frame.

The other response is the resistance mind frame. In this mind frame, people start attacking themselves for having the idea of "I can't do this" in the first place. The little voice inside your head may say something like "You coward, so and so has done it many times before."

Whatever response you have it leads to an internal war against yourself.

Remember the three magic questions:

1. Is this frame beneficial?

2. What is a better mind frame in this specific situation?

3. What can I do to make it real?

Don't feel ashamed about your self-limiting frames. We all have them! In a sense, they are a natural process in which your mind tries to 'protect' you. So accept that you suffer from a self-limiting perception; it is not the ultimate evil. Then acknowledge if it is not benefitting you in any way and try and change it.

You have probably heard the saying: "What you resist persists, what you accept you gain the power to control." The same applies to your self-limiting frames.

Incidentally, whenever you, or a client, say: "I can't do it", add the word "yet" to the end of the sentence. It completely changes the emphasis from a negative to an empowering position. It is also a great technique to teach your children!

In this chapter we have touched on profound truths with regards to your perception and how to change it. These are very important principles to Radical Coaching.

CHAPTER 13: THE THREE PRINCIPLES

"You're always only one thought away from happiness, and always only one thought away from sadness." Sydney Banks

History of the Three Principles

As a Radical Coach, you need to know about the Three Principles so as to understand their influence on Radical Coaching.

William James was one of the founders of the field of psychology. Over a century ago, he awaited the discovery of a set of principles that could explain all human behavior. James felt that following these principles could lead an individual to reach a higher level of well-being (SydneyBanks.org; 2010).

As fate would have it, it was not a psychologist, or even any other educated person who had the revelation. (This will not be a surprise to Radical Coaches who know that all people have unlimited potential!)

Sydney Banks was a migrant from Scotland who settled in Canada. In 1973, he and his wife attended an Encounter Group event for couples in an attempt to mend their marriage. At this event, he met a psychologist with whom he discussed his past as an orphan, his lack of education and his general dissatisfaction with life. The psychologist responded saying that all of Sydney Banks's discontentment and unhappiness were just a result of his thoughts; nothing more. (Rees-Evans; 2011)

This reply left Banks sleepless for several nights, pondering the real power of thought. Banks then had an epiphany that made him realize that reality is created by the Three Principles of Mind, Consciousness and Thought. Banks understood the Three Principles as follows:

- 'Mind' as the source of all intelligence
- 'Consciousness' as that which makes us aware of our existence
- 'Thought' as the guide which leads through life with the gift of being free-thinkers. It is the steering wheel which guides us through life using the intelligence of 'Mind' and the awareness of 'Consciousness.' (Rees-Evans; 2011)

This new understanding led Banks to become more content with himself and life in general. His old shy, insecure characteristics were replaced by a confident person with great wisdom and vitality.

Life seemed to continue as normal. Once Banks started sharing his new insights, he realized that the principles brought about a change in other people too. In general, people were feeling more relaxed and their relationships improved. Physically people felt healthier.

It wasn't long before news spread of Banks' life changing wisdom. People from all over the world began to visit him, wanting to learn more about his Three Principles. Even Buddhist Monks from Tibet were interested in what he had to say (Rees-Evans; 2011).

At this time, two psychologist Dr. Roger Mills and Dr. George Pransky, were considering the promotion of mental health as an alternative to treating pathology. Soon they heard about the work of Sydney Banks. They were especially amazed at an uneducated man's ability to influence so many people in such a positive way (Rees-Evans; 2011).

Sydney Banks' Three Principles directly opposed all that these psychologists had been taught at University and in the beginning they felt offended by his ideas. However, it was only a matter of time before they started noticing changes within themselves as they spent more and more time learning from Banks (Rees-Evans; 2011).

They decided to test Banks' ideas with experiments and they were dumbfounded by the exceptional results. The 'new' psychology didn't take off at first. People found it too 'mysterious', but the psychologists had enough participants in their experiments to obtain the necessary data they were looking for (Rees-Evans; 2011).

According to his research, Mills concluded that if people can understand the power of their thoughts they will start controlling the response to their thoughts more wisely. Banks felt it was impossible to have an emotion without having a thought first and Mills further explored this theory.

He later concluded that it is not emotions that are stored in memory, but rather thoughts. These thoughts lead to certain emotions which then influence our experience of life (Rees-Evans; 2011).

Further studies by Mills and Pransky also proved that mental health was not just the absence of illness. Instead they found that mental health can reach higher levels of well-being than ever known before. The Three Principles found their way into the field of psychology and has been studied ever since (Rees-Evans; 2011).

What are the Three Principles?

The Three Principles were first described by Sydney Banks. Later on other names emerged like Innate Health or Health Realization. Basically it relies on the assumption that all people are innately psychologically healthy. They can choose to experience this mental health any time they choose to (SydneyBanks.org; 2010).

As a coach you will achieve far greater success with your clients once you learn to see them as healthy individuals. According to the Three Principles, clients are not broken people who need to be fixed, they just have faulty thinking.

Sydney Banks' Three Principles of Mind, Consciousness and Thought

Sydney Banks recognized the close relationship between mind, consciousness and thought.

If you, as a coach, can teach your clients to use 'Thought' properly, they will lead a better life than they ever dreamed of. This ability could lead to joy as well as the freedom from illusionary unhappiness. The best way to deal with unhappiness is to recognize it for what it truly is – just 'Thought.'

Radical Coaching helps people to understand that the source of their unhappiness is nothing other than 'Thought.' It further brings them back to the present time in which they may indeed be happy.

The principles rely on "spiritual knowledge" which essentially means that you will find what you are looking for once you are ready to receive it. Everybody has an equal ability to obtain this spiritual knowledge. This equality comes from the fact that all people have access to Mind, Consciousness and Thought (Kelley; 2003).

Radical Coaching recognizes the ability of all people to lead happy and fulfilled lives. Further, it recognizes that given a free choice, people will choose to do the thing that makes them feel good.

Mind

Eastern Philosophers have a saying: 'Big Mind, Little Mind.' The Little Mind refers to the self-centered ego while the Big Mind refers to the Divine or Universal Mind. Big Mind is considered to be the origin of all intelligence in the world. It is also seen as the only Mind with the power to lead you through life. This implies that the origin of happiness does not lie on the outside, but on the inside (SydneyBanks.org; 2010).

'Mind' is regarded as the ultimate life force or the energy of life. It affects thought and consciousness in such a way as to continuously create experiences that are perceived as 'reality.' Thought and Consciousness are therefore only psychological functions set in motion by Mind and they are the proof of Mind in action (Kelley; 2003).

Teaching your clients how to use the Big Mind can help them to create better realities. It will also help them to hold higher views and opinions of themselves as well as others.

Radical Coaches have to guard themselves against their Little Minds. They have to ensure that they never act in an arrogant way or from feelings of superiority, regardless of the client's social, educational or financial standing. This will be a direct contradiction of exactly what Radical Coaching is.

Consciousness

According to Sydney Banks, 'Consciousness' is what helps us to realize that life exists. Consciousness can be experienced at an unlimited number of levels that never reach an end. This implies that the possibilities of finding splendor, love and understanding are endless. There is no excuse to stagnate, only the prospect of growth. The secret to constantly growing is to not work at it (Rees-Evans; 2011).

Radical Coaching knows that everybody has access to a Divine secret that has been known to all the wise men from the beginning of time. The secret is that everything your clients are looking for is already inside of them. You have the privilege of sharing this secret with every client and opening up their eyes to this truth (Rees-Evans; 2011).

Radical Coaches have the ability to guide their clients towards a higher level of consciousness. The higher their level of consciousness, the greater will be their understanding. This in turn will allow them to access more wisdom and common sense. Once they reach a higher level of consciousness, they will be able to see past whatever illusion obscured their view previously (Kelley; 2003).

Ultimately it is your client's consciousness that will give rise to their thoughts. Consciousness transforms thoughts into subjective experience through the physical senses. Consciousness is the on-going sensory experience of thought.

I hope this is making you very excited! It implies that every client will constantly be a masterpiece forever in the making. Expect surprises! Expect miracles! If your clients choose to carry on with this path, they will be transformed from glory to glory right before your eyes. And the best thing about it all? It's a show that will never stop!

Thought

Sydney Banks emphasized a very important point: "You're always only one thought away from happiness, and always only one thought away from sadness. It is therefore clear to see that the secret to happiness lies in thought. He described it as the 'missing link' everybody in the world is looking for." This is a great part of the results that clients are looking for from coaches (SydneyBanks.org; 2010).

Have you ever noticed how much time we spend worrying over nothing? Often we will look back into our past and not know why we ever worried about a certain thing. And often, a few days after an angry fit you can't even remember what you were mad about. All these worries and anger are nothing but just thoughts. Often we can't even remember what the thoughts were that led to these actions.

Forgiving means letting go of negative thoughts, whether it be negative thoughts about someone else or negative thoughts about ourselves. Some of your clients may need to forgive themselves for whatever mistakes they felt they made in the past.

We were all given the divine gift of walking through life and seeing just what we want to see. It is called the gift of free thinking (Rees-Evans; 2011).

We were also given the ability to act on our thoughts. However, having the gift of free thinking does not mean that we can act freely without considering the consequences. Our actions are the ways in which we give life to our thoughts (Rees-Evans; 2011). A Radical Coach will aid his or her clients in carefully considering the consequences of their actions as these are birthed from thought.

Thought is the imaging ability of each individual or that which accounts for all mental activity. Thought is the continuous creation of "reality" through the process of mental activity (Rees-Evans; 2011). If you can teach a client to control how they react to their thoughts, you can ultimately help them create a new world, or a new reality.

CHAPTER 14: THE POTENTIAL OF THE THREE PRINCIPLES IN RADICAL COACHING

"To look outside for the answers you seek is to dream. To look within is to awaken the wisdom that lies within." Sydney Banks

When people approach a coach, it is usually because they want to change something in their lives so that they can get better results than they are currently getting. They are not happy and they are struggling to change things on their own.

To put it slightly differently, the reason why people turn to coaches is not because they want an ear to listen to them or a shoulder to cry on; they want results. They want to change something. They want to be a different person after they met you than they were before they met you. They want a future that is different from their default future!

People are buckling under the pressure of their careers. Children lack motivation at school. In general, there appears to be an increasing feeling of discontent with life amongst young and old alike.

A person's every achievement may become a standard that needs to be exceeded the next time around, leading to an ever-increasing amount of tension. For example, this is often the Elephant in the Room for the top performing salespeople in organizations. They have a great year but then have to start the next year from zero. They often ask themselves: "What if I can't manage to do it again?" "What if I disappoint my manager or even myself?"

The constant fear of not being able to deliver can easily deprive people of their joy of living. If this fear is further strengthened by the fear of losing everything they have worked so hard for, then their lives can end up feeling like a jail sentence, instead of an exciting adventure.

Remember the old tale: "If you love something, set it free. If it comes back to you, it is yours; if it doesn't, it never was." You can never lose that which truly belongs to you.

As a Radical Coach you need to fight the lie that tells your clients that by improving the outside, they can improve the inside. The truth is the exact opposite - it is the inside world that affects the outside world.

As I am writing this in September 2013, I've just read a Facebook message from a client who wrote about her struggle with a skin condition:

"When my inside changed, my outside started to change."

Several studies have proven the effectiveness of the Three Principles in improving people's emotional, spiritual and physical well-being. It makes sense therefore for a Radical Coach to know how to use it to help his or her clients.

Help your clients understand the endless creative capacity of their own minds and they will create a better reality than the one they feel trapped in now. They will never again focus on the outside world as an option for improving their inner self.

But the Three Principles have even further reaching potential than just improving the self.

Pransky realized that when people are influenced by the teaching of the Three Principles, they spontaneously begin to positively affect their communities or workplaces. In the same way, Radical Coaching can help individuals and companies to reach new heights.

Radical Business Coaching can influence a firm in a positive way. It will help staff members achieve their potential and their ability to affect the success and future growth of the company.

This way the Three Principles might have a ripple effect reaching far more than just a few individuals.

Reporting on some of the findings in his studies Pransky stated: "Clearly, something had happened to them of such magnitude that their lives would never be the same. They would never turn back." (Rees-Evans; 2011)

And that is exactly what clients are paying coaches for – lasting results!

Long term, positive change can only be achieved when an individual's thinking changes from a negative direction into a new, positive direction. As each individual possesses all the qualities needed to make this change, no one has an excuse for being miserable forever.

Other studies that explore the effect of the Three Principles in troubled communities deliver the following results:

- 43% decrease in violence;

- 38% decrease in drug and alcohol related crimes;

- 25% decrease in sexually transmitted disease incidences;

- 40% reduction in domestic violence and child abuse cases;

- A 35% reduction in the overall crime rate;

- A 25% decrease in teen pregnancy;

- A 32% increase in health screening;

- A 30% drop in the unemployment rate;

- A 40% drop in school absence and failure;

- 87% of parents reporting that their children were more cooperative;

- Parents being less frustrated with their children and less hostile towards them;

- An increase of 60% in the household employment rate;

- A 75% decrease in school discipline referrals and suspensions;
- A 500% increase in parents' school involvement (Rees-Evans; 2011) (Kelley; 2003).

Wow! The results speak for themselves. Can any Radical Coach afford not to take note of the Three Principles?

In essence, Sydney Banks' Three Principles are an attempt to direct a person back to their innate state of well-being. This is done by revealing how their reality is created in an instant through their own thoughts, and nothing more. Their state of well-being is therefore in their own hands (or rather their own heads) and in nobody else's.

A Radical Coach can empower people to continuously better their own state of well-being. For example, help them to see that just because anger entered their minds, they didn't have to react to it. It was their choice!

Similarly, just because someone did something that caused the client to feel upset, it was their choice whether to react to the upsetting behavior. Their choice either increased tension or decreased the tension.

People who display a high level of well-being are usually confident, outgoing, peaceful, enthusiastic and resourceful. These individuals usually experience more positive emotions and display matching positive behavioral patterns. They will usually err on the optimistic side and their stored memories tend to be positive (Rees-Evans; 2011).

The physical advantages of a high level of well-being must also not be ignored. Sensations like pain are less severe in people with high well-being levels due to less bodily tension. They also experience better physical health than those with lower levels of well-being and display better social skills (Kelley; 2003).

Research has proven time and time again that children with a healthier mental state and positive outlook on life do better at school. They also continue their studies further than those with lower levels of mental well-being. This implies that the Three Principles can help children to reach their full potential and lead significant lives in which they can contribute positively to society (Rees-Evans; 2011).

Some studies have also shown that challenges like teen pregnancy, drug abuse and low education levels are not a result of psychological pathology. It would appear that instead, these occur due to a lack of contentment and common sense. The Three Principles can therefore be highly beneficial in the adolescent years (Rees-Evans; 2011).

The above are not only the results clients are looking for in their own lives, workplaces and communities. It is also what makes the profession of coaching such a rewarding one.

CHAPTER 15: POSITIVE PSYCHOLOGY - THE POWER OF EMOTIONS

"When we live in self-alignment, our inner guidance system is trustworthy. Looking outside of ourselves for validation, acceptance and security dilutes this self-trust. There are simply too many expectations projected upon us that do not align with the evolution of our own unique ways of being ourselves in the world."
Sirah Vettese

Positive Psychology is a systematic study of positive life-events, positive individual characteristics and those things that assist in their development.

A coach needs to understand that clients do not just want to be free from worry and sadness. Clients want to be content and happy, enjoying a life of meaning and purpose.

Positive Psychology is concerned with a focus on the positive attributes of life. Many studies have revealed that it may also lead to resilience against the onset of mental disease.

History of Positive Psychology

The roots of Positive Psychology date as far back as the time of Socrates, Plato and Aristotle. These philosophers were already curious about the origin of the 'good life.'

During the eighteenth and nineteenth centuries, other psychological theories like psychoanalysis, behaviorism, cognitive therapy, humanistic psychology and existential psychology made their appearance. All of these modalities studied the positive characteristics of human beings and their daily lives (Duckworth et al; 2005).

Then came World War II, with all its destruction, poverty, high unemployment rate and of course severe trauma, both physically and mentally. This left many people scarred and unable to cope with what remained after the war (Seligman & Csikszentmihalyi; 2000).

From a psychological perspective, the simple antidote was to identify and treat whatever mental illnesses resulted from the traumatic global event. This is not necessarily a bad thing. Our knowledge of potentially life threatening mental illnesses as well as their treatment expanded beyond expectation (Seligman & Csikszentmihalyi; 2000).

New psychotherapies evolved that often delivered better results than medication. For example, we now know of the influence of genes on the possible development of mental disorders. We also know of environmental triggers such as divorce, retrenchment, exposure to heavy metal toxins and poverty (Seligman & Csikszentmihalyi; 2000).

Unfortunately, this has neglected the other side of human existence. Humans possess many positive traits that enable them to overcome adversity and prosper in spite of it. The 'build-on-what's-strong' approach was forgotten for the sake of the 'fix-what's-wrong' approach (Seligman & Csikszentmihalyi; 2000).

Humanistic psychology probably has the closest resemblance to Positive Psychology. Both are concerned with asking the same questions: "When is life good?", "When do individuals perform at their best?", "How can we help ourselves and other to grow?", "What does it mean to be real?"

It was during the 50's and 60's that Humanistic Psychology became a much talked about topic and the works of Carl Rogers, Abraham Maslow, Henry Murray, Gordon Allport and Rollo May contributed to its popularity (Seligman & Csikszentmihalyi; 2000).

In the late 50's, Marie Jahoda wrote a book – Current Concepts of Positive Mental Health. In this book she identifies six processes that contribute to mental health instead of mental illness:

1. Self-acceptance

2. Growth

3. Incorporation of personality

4. Self-government

5. Perceiving reality accurately

6. Mastering the environment

During the 80's and 90's, a similar survey was conducted amongst different theorists of what they have identified as the building blocks of well-being. The results closely resembled what Jahoda had written in her book (Duckworth et al; 2005).

Early in this century, scientists uncovered the link between positive human experience and biological processes within the human body.

Radical Coaching views the client as a whole person, incorporating mind, emotions, soul and body. This means we always aim to help clients in their entirety and not just zoom in on one aspect of their being.

The advocates of Positive Psychology hope to rebalance the scale between mental health and mental illness. This is done through the study of positive characteristics, welfare and ideal functioning. Even people who suffer from mental illness still have access to their inner ability to overcome hardship and change their circumstances (Seligman & Csikszentmihalyi; 2000).

As I've mentioned before, in Radical Coaching there is no such thing as a 'broken' client who needs to be 'fixed.' Each individual is, or can become, a strong, capable ruler over his or her own life.

How does Positive Psychology Work?

As a scientific field of study, Positive Psychology aims to achieve measurable outcomes of the positive attributes of human experience.

Positive Psychology is considered to be a scientific modality. It consequently emphasizes the importance of objective and accurate measures to determine its validity and efficacy. However, as Positive Psychology is still a relatively new theory, it has not been studied to the same extent as other psychological theories (Seligman & Csikszentmihalyi; 2000).

Three categories were identified as requirements for mental well-being: the pleasant life, the engaged life and the meaningful life.

The Pleasant Life

This category considers people's emotions relating to their present, past and future experiences. Some of the characteristics of a positive life are:

Typical positive emotions rooted in the past that include gratification, tranquility and fulfillment.

Present positive emotions may rely on the fulfillment of momentary sensory desires as well as more complex pleasure which require some form of learning.

Optimism, hope and faith are positive emotions related to the future.

In this life, a person experiences the maximum positive experiences and the minimum pain and negativity.

Radical Coaching aims to enable a person to experience the pleasures of their current life. It helps clients to build these pleasant experiences onto the positive foundations of the past and keeps them motivated with positive future images (Seligman & Csikszentmihalyi; 2000).

Engaged Life

This category is characterized by positive character and talents.

Qualities that are considered valuable across many cultural and historical boundaries are what contribute to strength of character. These qualities are courage, leadership, compassion, integrity, creativity, wisdom and love.

Combining their strong character with their talents, clients may experience more commitment, interest and flow.

A coach should always search for and support the greatness in people. This is what will enable their clients to overcome any obstacle and reach their full potential (Seligman & Csikszentmihalyi; 2000).

Meaningful Life

People who live fulfilling, happy, lives usually have a bigger, higher purpose. These elements may include mentoring, being part of a strong family or community, living in a democracy and having freedom of speech.

None of us are islands and we do not function optimally in isolation. As a coach, your aim is to help your clients be part of some form of 'community.' This community may exist in their workplace or at home (Seligman & Csikszentmihalyi; 2000).

Measuring Subjective Well-being

Subjective well-being is seen as "a person's cognitive and affective evaluations of his or her own life". I had to read this several times to make sense of it so if you want the short version, "your subjective well-being relates to your self-worth!" The components of well-being are the experience of positive emotion, the lack of negative emotion and a perceptible finding of contentment and inner peace.

Positive Psychology wants to measure well-being. This helps to focus the attention of both the client and the coach on the possibly neglected positive resources available to coaching.

For research purposes, measuring well-being can give a more complete image of any psychological processes influencing disorders.

You can get free access to self-assessment questionnaires through free registration at the University of Pennsylvania's Authentic Happiness website:
http://www.authentichappiness.sas.upenn.edu/Default.aspx

It should probably be mentioned that the accuracy of self-assessment questionnaires may be influenced by an individual's fluctuating mood. I therefore strongly recommend that you use a multi method approach to ensure accurate results (Seligman & Csikszentmihalyi; 2000).

Measuring Strength of Character

The second happy life of Positive Psychology, the engaged life, requires people to use their strengths and talents to create flow. For this reason, it ought to be possible to measure the relevant positive individual traits which include gifts, interests and strengths.

To make it easier to measure strengths, they are classified into six categories obtained from continuous historical data. These six are wisdom and understanding, valor, love, righteousness, self-restraint and wholeness (Seligman & Csikszentmihalyi; 2000).

Measuring Engagement and Flow

Living an engaged life requires the use of an individual's strengths and gifts to overcome obstacles in life.

Engagement differs from pleasure in that its quality makes it a different sort of satisfaction. Flow is what results from someone engaging their strengths and gifts to overcome what appears at first to be an insurmountable challenge. This idea can be best described as focusing so much on the task at hand that you become unaware of your surroundings. It feels as if time has stopped and your concentration levels are at their peak, yet you feel comfortable and relax in this state.

Flow is usually thought to be empty of thought and emotion. The void is caused by all psychological processes focusing on the task at hand and not on creating non-relevant thoughts or emotions. Sports people call it "Being in the Zone."

The experience sampling method or ESM is the most widely used measuring tool for flow. This method is applied by a coach contacting subjects at multiple and random intervals. The clients are asked to fill out questionnaires at that time.

In this way it does not rely on retrospective evaluation alone and it takes the current patterns in daily behavior and experience into account (Seligman & Csikszentmihalyi; 2000).

Measuring Meaning

The meaningful life, or third happy life, aims to serve something bigger than oneself. This is one of the core issues a Radical Coach works on with clients – helping the latter to find, and connect with, that bigger 'something.'

This 'something' that people choose to connect with, varies widely amongst individuals. It may be anything ranging from family, friends and church to work or some serious calling.

People seldom derive meaning from just one single source. Instead, they choose to become attached to multiple and varied 'higher' purposes.

Because of the elements of the meaningful life, it is often difficult to measure meaning. It is usually an open-ended measurement.

One way of attempting to measure meaning is through conducting interviews that aim to explore a variety of topics.

One of the techniques I have used is to ask clients to write the story of their lives as if it were a book. I ask them to describe the significant happenings in their lives as specific chapters in this book. These chapters may describe a high point, a low point, a turning point, their earliest memory, significant occurrences in their childhood, teenage years and adult life.

Ask clients to give some more information on important 'characters' in the book. They may also give some information on future chapters. I usually ask them to right the story in the 3rd person, as if describing someone else.

Questions about the message conveyed in the 'book' often give a coach significant insight into what the client considers to be important.

The physical and psychological benefits of writing about a traumatic event have long been known. Evidence is only now growing about what happens when people narrate, either verbally or in writing, their most positive experiences in life (Duckworth et al; 2005).

Another way at looking at the three 'lives' of positive psychology is in the form of three of my favorite questions:

1. Have I lived life to the full?

2. Have I loved and been loved?

3. Have I made a difference?

Rather than this being your epitaph, ask these questions now and act upon them!

This leads to my personal motto: "Live, Love, Make a Difference!"

CHAPTER 16: THE POTENTIAL OF POSITIVE PSYCHOLOGY IN RADICAL COACHING

"What contributes to the success of 'high' functioning people?"
Margaret Moore

In Radical Coaching, we believe that the primary purpose of coaching is to help a client become happier and more fulfilled by getting the results they are seeking. Emphasizing the positive is a key way to do this.

There is evidence that suggests that positive emotions have the ability to 'undo' some negative emotions. Studies have shown how positive emotions can alleviate the cardiovascular effects caused by negative emotions (a rapid heartbeat, raised blood pressure, and contraction of blood vessels). (Duckworth et al; 2005).

Recent studies have also demonstrated how positive emotions may help individuals to find a positive purpose behind stressful situations or hardships. This is demonstrated in what is called the 'upward spiral' of positive emotion. As people with positive emotions find positive reasons behind negative events, their positive emotions increase even further. This gives them some form of resilience against negative experiences that can counteract the development of mental illnesses like stress and depression (Duckworth et al; 2005).

Evidence-based studies done on the role of positive interventions have delivered promising results. Most of the positive interventions are based on Fordyce's principle that "happy is as happy does." According to this principle, positive emotions lead to the development of positive habits.

Some of the positive interventions that were tested on college students included keeping busy, being more active and socializing. The results were that students were happier and suffered less from anxiety and depression at the end of the term than students in the control group. What is even more impressive is that the results were maintained between 9 and 18 months later (Duckworth et al; 2005).

The intervention of writing about positive emotions was also put to the test. Students in the intervention group experienced better moods and became sick less often than those students in the control group.

Another example of positive intervention is to keep a gratitude, or a 'count your blessings' journal. Students in the intervention group felt more optimistic and better connected to others compared to those students in the control group (Duckworth et al; 2005).

Another study that focused on this intervention reported that counting your blessings once a week delivered better results than doing it every day. Doing it too regularly may lead to adaptation and less emotional involvement as a result (Duckworth et al; 2005).

Acts of kindness have also been studied as positive intervention. As in the study above, performing acts of kindness all in one day instead of everyday prevented adaptation. It also kept the test subjects emotionally involved (Duckworth et al; 2005).

A small study has even been conducted on test subjects who suffered from depression. They all had confirmed depression. Their depression was confirmed according to the Beck Depression Index and their depression was further evaluated against the Hamilton Rating Scale of Depression.

After a 15 week period of reading and discussing positive strategies to increase their enjoyment of life, none of them met the criteria for depression anymore! (Duckworth et al; 2005).

CHAPTER 17: EMOTIONAL INTELLIGENCE

"Societies can be sunk by the weight of buried ugliness."
Daniel Goleman

Another important influence on Radical Coaching is Emotional Intelligence, a skill that helps you to become aware of and understand your own and others' emotions. This skill has many benefits:

- It helps to manage stress in a positive way.
- It facilitates effective communication amongst individuals.
- It helps you to have empathy with other.
- It aids in overcoming difficult challenges.
- It can help neutralize conflict (Segal & Smith; 2013).

It is emotional intelligence that determines your approachability or how easily people are drawn to you.

Emotional intelligence depends on four abilities; the ability to perceive emotions, reason with emotions and the ability to understand and manage emotions.

Emotional Perception

Emotions may be perceived through verbal as well as non-verbal cues. Verbal cues may include the tone of a person's voice, while non-verbal cues refer to facial expressions and body language (Mayer, et al; n.d).

Emotional Reasoning

This ability refers to whether you can incorporate your own and others' emotions into your thinking and decision making process. In other words how you prioritize your attention based on the emotional input you receive (Mayer, et al; n.d).

Emotional Understanding

This refers to seeing the reasons behind your own and others' emotional response. In a sense it means that you should be able to accurately interpret other's emotions. This interpretation is important to gain more information like the cause of the emotions (Mayer, et al; n.d).

Emotional Management

This is actually what emotional intelligence is all about. It is the ability to use emotions in a positive way to either improve your own or others' life. This includes the ability to control your own emotions so that you can respond in an appropriate way to others' emotions (Mayer, et al; n.d).

The History of Emotional Intelligence

Edward Thorndike was the first to touch on the subject when he referred to 'social intelligence' in the 1930's. According to him social intelligence refers to the talent of getting along well with other people (Cherry; n.d).

During the 1940's David Wechsler studied the emotional aspects of intelligence and considered that it may indeed be necessary to achieve success (Cherry; n.d).

In the 1950's, Abraham Maslow, a humanistic psychologist, indicated that it was indeed possible for people to increase their emotional strength (Cherry; n.d).

Howard Gardner published his "The Shattered Mind" in 1975 which explores the existence of different types of intelligence (Cherry; n.d).

The term "emotional intelligence" was used for the first time by Wayne Payne in his doctoral thesis published in 1985. Two years later, in 1987, Keith Beasley refers to the "emotional quotient" in an article written for Mensa Magazine (Cherry; n.d).

It was only during the 1990's that emotional intelligence gained popularity through the work of two psychologists, Peter Salovey and John Mayer. Together they published their groundbreaking article "Emotional Intelligence". In 1995, Daniel Goleman published the first book on emotional intelligence called "Emotional Intelligence: Why it Can Matter More than IQ." (Cherry; n.d)

Why is Emotional Intelligence Important?

There have been many claims that emotional intelligence is a better predictor of success in future life than IQ. Since emotional intelligence is still a relatively new theory, these claims are not yet supported by any physical studies (Mayer, et al; n.d).

Some studies that have been conducted on emotional intelligence so far, which have shown the following benefits, as seen in individuals with a high EQ:

- High EQ individuals have better problem solving skills when it comes to emotional problems.

- These people also tend to have higher levels of other intelligences including higher social and verbal intelligence.

- High EQ people are more approachable and agreeable than people with a lower EQ.

- They are more prone to follow 'social' careers, like teaching or counseling.

- They are less prone to self-destructive behavior like smoking, drinking, drug abusive and aggressive relationships.

- High EQ people also have a better idea about their future goals (Segal & Smith; 2013).

It has also been suggested that groups who exhibit higher levels of emotional intelligence tend to be less aggressive (Mayer, et al; n.d). This may just bring about the 'world peace' that every beauty queen has been after for so long!

This does not however, imply that emotional intelligence is the only predictor for success in life. There are many positive qualities that can add to an individual's chances of success and emotional intelligence is but one.

How is EQ measured?

"In regard to measuring emotional intelligence – I am a great believer that criterion-report (that is, ability testing) is the only adequate method to employ. Intelligence is an ability and is directly measured only by having people answer questions and evaluating the correctness of those answers." --John D. Mayer

As with most intelligence screening test, questionnaires are used to determine an individual's EQ. There are four tests that help to identify an individual's EQ.

1. Reuven Bar-On's EQ-i

This is a self-assessment questionnaire which focuses on skills like awareness, the ease of stress management, problem solving skills and overall happiness (Cherry; n.d).

"Emotional intelligence is an array of non-cognitive capabilities, competencies, and skills that influence one's ability to succeed in coping with environmental demands and pressures." – Bar-On.

2. Multifactor Emotional Intelligence Scale (MEIS)

This test employs simple tasks in order to determine an individual's emotional intelligence. These tasks are aimed at determining a person's ability to perceive, recognize, understand and manage their emotions, based on the four subcategories of emotional intelligence (Cherry; n.d).

3. Seligman Attribution Style Questionnaire (SASQ)

This test was originally developed for Metropolitan Life Insurance Company to indicate a person's level of optimism and pessimism (Cherry; n.d).

4. Emotional Competence Inventory (ECI)

This is a questionnaire for the acquaintances of a specific individual. The questionnaire scores their various emotional abilities (Cherry; n.d).

CHAPTER 18: THE IMPORTANCE OF EMOTIONAL INTELLIGENCE IN RADICAL COACHING

"If your emotional abilities aren't in hand, if you don't have self-awareness, if you are not able to manage your distressing emotions, if you can't have empathy and have effective relationships, then no matter how smart you are, you are not going to get very far."
Daniel Goleman

In this book we have touched on the importance of emotions many times and we will be looking at the topic again later on. It should really not be a mystery anymore why emotional intelligence would be important in Radical Coaching.

It is important for a Radical Coach to possess a high level of emotional intelligence. It will help you to 'read' your clients' emotions accurately and respond in an appropriate way. This chapter is in fact more important to you as a coach than to your clients. At the end of the chapter is an exercise to help you with this skill.

As a coach you need to be able to clarify what lies behind your clients' emotions. Since people are all different, a specific emotion in one person might have a completely different cause than in another person. Never assume – if you have any doubts, ask questions.

As a Radical Coach, be aware of the fact that you will be working a lot with clients' emotions. If this is something you feel uncomfortable with, perhaps you need to reconsider your choice of career!

Whether it is possible for an individual to reach a higher level of emotional intelligence remains a controversial subject. Researchers mostly agree that it is possible to increase your emotional knowledge to a great extent (Mayer, et al; n.d).

The reason behind this controversy is that any type of intelligence refers to a person's capacity or potential for intelligence. No study exists to prove that you can indeed increase the capacity for any type of intelligence, including emotional intelligence (Mayer, et al; n.d).

You can however develop the existing potential to its fullest. Emotional knowledge is what emotional intelligence operates on and it is indeed possible to increase that.

Increasing your Emotional Knowledge

There are five skills that you can acquire which will help you increase your emotional knowledge.

Skill #1: Reducing Stress

There are three simple steps which can help you identify and overcome stress.

1. **Recognize stress** – Become aware of what stress feels like for you. Do you suffer from tense muscles, feeling out of breath or a burning sensation over your tummy? Stress usually has some physical effect. In order to help you recognize the presence of stress, you need to know your symptoms and to understand that they can change over time. My symptoms used to be felt in my tummy – now, it's a tension at the back of my neck. There's no rationale that I can identify for the change – it is what it is.

2. **Identify your stress reaction** - Do you become angry or irritated once you feel stressed? This is necessary to identify your best stress relief methods. If you become agitated you will need stress relief that calms you down. If you feel depressed because of stress you will need some form of positive stimulation. For example, even though I've successfully run management training courses for over 30 years, and been coaching for even longer, before I work with a new client, I always have a strong desire for them to postpone the work. I've come to recognize that this is my symptom of stress and now, I almost welcome it!

3. **Identify the appropriate stress relief actions for you** - The best way to reduce stress is to involve your senses in the action. If you are visually stimulated, look at a calming picture of the ocean. If you are stimulated by sound, play some relaxing music to help you relax. (Segal & Smith; 2013).

Skill # 2: Emotional Awareness

Many people have learned how to suppress their emotions. In order for you to develop your emotional intelligence to its highest potential, you may need to dust off these emotions. It may not be a pleasant discovery. To become more aware of your emotions consider the following questions:

- Do emotions play a role in every part of your day? Are you excited in the morning when you wake up? Frustrated in traffic? Angry at your boss? Glad to go home at the end of the day, etc?
- Do your emotions lead to physical sensations?
- Do certain subtle emotions show on your facial expression?
- Are your feelings sometimes so intense that you and other people take notice of them?
- Are you even aware of the fact that you are experiencing emotions? (Segal & Smith; 2013)

Skill # 3: Non-verbal Communication

What you say is often not as important as how you say it. Your gestures and facial expressions say just as much as your words. Even when you are silent, your body language conveys a certain message to the people around you.

You can improve your emotional knowledge by becoming aware of other people as well as your own non-verbal cues. The following tips can help you to improve your non-verbal communication:

- Pay attention to the other person – If your attention is not focused on the other person you will miss out on any non-verbal cues as well as possibly some important verbal ones too.

- Eye contact – This way you will appear interested in what the other person is saying. It will make them more likely to continue talking to you. It will also help you to notice any facial expression which my convey something about their emotional state.

- Look out for non-verbal cues – Be aware of your own as well as the other person's non-verbal cues. Notice how slow or fast the conversation is, their facial expression or body language and their tone of voice.

- Be aware of your own body language. For example, be wary of crossing your arms across your chest. Some people will interpret it as you feeling threatened or that you have withdrawn from the conversation (Segal & Smith; 2013).

Skill # 4: Apply humor and fun to challenging moments

Laughter reduces stress and keeps your senses clear so use these when dealing with difficult situations.

Keeping your communications light and playful has the following benefits:

- It makes the hard times more bearable.

- It takes the sharp edge off differences.

- It can help you to relax and even give you more energy.

- It adds to your creativity which can help you solve a problem faster.

You can learn to become more playful by making it a part of your everyday life. Take part in fun, enjoyable activities on a daily basis. Embrace your inner child by playing with animals or small children.

However, it is important to use your discretion. Humor is inappropriate if it may be interpreted as trivializing the situation (Segal & Smith; 2013).

Skill #5: Positive Conflict Resolution

The following are tips for managing conflict and building trust:

- Leave the old issues in the past. Keep your attention focused on the present problem. Let go of resentment and bitterness caused by previous conflicts as these may cloud your judgment in future.

- Pick your fights. Rate your arguments. Don't fight over things that are not important; arguments are time consuming and drain you of your energy. Make sure you are fighting for a good cause if you choose to fight.

- Don't seek revenge. This will only have you running around in circles and is very counterproductive. Choose to forgive and forget and get on with your life.

- Sometimes you must agree to disagree. If you see a conflict will not be resolved don't waste unnecessary time on it. Just walk away. It does not mean that you have to agree, you just have to withdraw from the argument (Segal & Smith; 2013).

It is very important for a Radical Coach to possess a high level of emotional intelligence. Just as important is to develop your emotional intelligence to its full potential.

CHAPTER 19: EMOTIONAL INTELLIGENCE EXERCISE

"People tend to become more emotionally intelligent as they age and mature." Daniel Goleman

This exercise is adapted from one I learned from Jonathan Altfeld who you can find at http://www.altfeld.com/mastery. He is a great NLP trainer and I recommend his courses to anyone wanting to learn NLP in an experiential way.

You need to find a partner to help you with this exercise.

Instructions:

1. Ask your partner 10 questions to which you know the answer to be 'yes'. They must answer truthfully. Look at them in slight peripheral vision and calibrate their non-verbal responses.

2. Now ask your partner another 10 questions to which you know that the answer is 'no'. This time, ask them to

lie by saying 'yes'. Identify the differences between step one and step two.

3. Now ask them questions to which you are not sure of the correct answer. They can answer truthfully or lie. You guess which. Check the accuracy of your guess with them after each one.

4. Turn yourself between each question so that your partner is in a different part of your visual field. Notice if this makes any difference to the accuracy of your guesses.

Questions

1. Could you tell when your partner was not telling the truth?

2. How did you know? (For example, did you notice changes in skin tone, breathing changes, changes in voice tonality or what else?)

3. Did you get any right without consciously being aware of any differences? (The non-conscious mind often notices more than we are consciously aware of).

4. Did you get it wrong 100% of the time? If you did, your non-conscious mind can still tell the difference but its message is being blocked by your conscious mind. All you have to do is say the opposite of what your conscious mind thinks is right!

CHAPTER 20: APPRECIATIVE INQUIRY – THE POWER OF WORDS

"Words Create Worlds." Title of a paper on Appreciative Inquiry

Listen carefully to the following words, so commonly used in the mental health profession: stressed, narcissism, anti-social personality, reactive depressive, type-A personality, obsessive compulsive, and codependent (Cooperrider & Whitney; n.d).

During the early days of psychology, these words were almost exclusively used by mental health professionals. These words have however become part of the average person's vocabulary. These days it is almost considered 'fashionable' to have some sort of mental disorder!

The big problem with a vocabulary like this is that it provides a person with both a label and an explanation for a problem. What makes it even worse is that often the mental disorder is traced back to something that happened in their past. Usually they had no control over it. They were helpless victims of an overprotective parent or an abusive childhood or something similar.

What makes this a dangerous approach is that it deprives people of control over their own lives. It makes them appear weak and consequently unable to escape this prison they are trapped in. It erodes people's power to create their own reality (Cooperrider & Whitney; n.d). This is of course nothing short of a lie, but it is a lie that many people choose to believe.

It also reinforces any tendency they may have to live their lives in victim mode, playing the blame game.

However, this does not just affect individual people. The vocabulary spreads from person to person. More people become victims of their past without the capacity to influence their own future. The number of people receiving treatment for mental disorders has increased exponentially in the short span of only a few years. This proves that a society's vocabulary can ultimately influence the future reality of that society (Cooperrider & Whitney; n.d).

Of course it is true that many of us, if not most of us, have had some very unpleasant experiences in our past. It definitely influenced us in some negative way at first, but that is not all we've got. We all have the capacity to feel good and be great. We can all achieve the extraordinary. We can change and influence the world around us and we can choose to live a better life in future.

There is a story, often told, that each human has been given two puppies to feed. One puppy is an evil puppy with the potential to destroy your life. The other is a good puppy, with the potential to make you prosper. The one you feed the most will ultimately become the stronger one and influence your life more than the other.

The above is a simple metaphor to illustrate that we all have positives and negatives at work in our lives. These include not only our own personal characteristics, but also past and present experiences which may have been either good or bad. The question is: which puppy do you choose to feed?

Popular psychological practice often uses words to focus a person's attention on what is wrong in their lives; on the negatives. What they are actually doing is feeding the evil puppy. They are not helping the individual to understand that they are the ones who have control over the puppy in the first place. They can choose to strengthen or weaken it. One coach said it another way: "When I gave my son a hammer, everything became a nail." (Cooperrider & Whitney; n.d)

Not only is this a very unproductive way of problem solving, it also adds to the ever increasing problem of human misery.

Appreciative Inquiry and Radical Coaching do exactly the opposite. They use positive words to focus a person's attention on the positives which may be positive characteristics or experiences.

These methods empower people. It reminds them of how they were capable of positively influencing their worlds in the past. It motivates them to keep on doing it in the future.

Below is a table highlighting the main differences between problem solving techniques and Appreciative Inquiry.

Problem Solving	**Appreciative Inquiry**
What problem should be fixed	What area needs to grow
Terminology used: fault, causes, treatment, symptoms, plan of action	Terminology used: what is already effective, what is good, what are the possibilities
Analysis and focuses on problems; ignores the positive, already effective aspects	Focuses on the positive, already effective aspects and tries to expand on the positive effect
Very slow process requiring huge amounts of positive energy to be spent	Generates energy to bring about fast changes
Views organizations as having mainly problems that need to be solved	Views organizations as centers of unlimited potential

(Coaching Leaders Ltd; 2012)

Appreciative Inquiry is one of the major influences on Radical Coaching. The philosophy of Appreciative Inquiry is closely related to Positive Psychology. Both focus on the positive and on creating an empowering and enriching image of the future.

It rejects the concept of clients presenting with problems that need solving. It concentrates immediately on what was already working well for the individual.

Radical Coaching, like Appreciative Inquiry, focuses on identifying and building on past and present successes. It also emphasizes reframing apparent negatives or failures, looking for the positive in them.

The History of Appreciative Inquiry

Appreciative Inquiry is only a few decades old. It was originally introduced in the eighties, by David Cooperrider and his colleagues at Case Western Reserve University.

Cooperrider's wife taught him about the 'appreciative eye' in the world of art which believes that every piece of art has beauty. He then started looking for the 'beauty' in every person and organization. This is how Appreciative Inquiry was born (Cooperrider & Whitney; n.d).

The theory that supports the development of Appreciative Inquiry is based on five principles:

1. The Constructionist Principle

This principle simply states that you can't separate human knowledge from organizational destiny. What people know will influence the world around them. More than that, it is a human being's knowledge that will lead to him or her creating or 'constructing' a certain reality.

In many ways, it is the organizational consequence of the premise than people's perception is their reality.

How we construct this world or reality relies strongly on the knowledge we have about people and our environment. We are all constantly busy constructing our realities. We need to continuously inquire, read and know the people and the world that surrounds us.

Radical Coaching and Appreciative Inquiry both acknowledge the part that 'knowing' plays in any attempt at change.

This process of knowing involves the following aspects:

- How do we know what we know?
- Whose opinions matter and whose do not?
- Is the world truly controlled by external laws, or do human choices and consequences indeed make a difference?
- What is the origin of knowledge? Does it lie in nature, structure or in the human mind?

Basically this principle replaces the individual, as the source of knowledge, with the relationship to others and the world. It acknowledges the influence of communication in creating human realities. It also recognizes the need to continuously inquire and improve these realities through language and communication (Cooperrider & Whitney; n.d).

2. The Simultaneity Principle

In short, this principle is about inquiry and change being simultaneous processes. Inquiry is considered to be nothing less than the seeds of change. Without inquiry there can be no change.

Inquiry involves the following:

- What do people think about?
- What do people talk about?
- What do people discover?
- What do they learn from these discoveries?
- How does this knowledge influence how and what they talk about?
- How does this knowledge change the way they see the future?

Radical Coaching and Appreciative Inquiry spend a lot of time asking questions, instead of providing answers. This principle of simultaneity indicates very well how just asking questions can already bring about positive change without necessarily requiring fixed, pre-determined answers.

At a non-conscious level, we are all aware of the profound impact of any kind of 'research.' Asking questions can draw our attention to a specific issue, characteristic or part of life that we have neglected. This type of research or asking questions can change our perception and consequently our reality in a heartbeat.

Even the most insignificant question can change our awareness, our conversations and our emotions (Cooperrider & Whitney; n.d).

3. The Poetic Principle

According to this principle, life is an open book, which is constantly being written by anyone and everyone who enter our reality. Everything is open to interpretation. The more people enter our world, the more possibilities exist for interpreting life and the world in a variety of ways.

However, not everybody's opinion will influence us which again leads us to the constructivist principle asking "Whose opinions matter and whose don't?" Chances are that we may still be influenced by people who interpret things differently than we do. This may increase our learning and ultimately our knowledge.

One of the main advantages of the poetic principle is that it prevents people from creating the same realities over and over again. It avoids the scenario of repeatedly asking the same questions.

Appreciative Inquiry and Radical Coaching acknowledge the fact that there are multiple outcomes to change and that the options are endless. As the questions change, the options change and consequently the realities change.

It would be foolish to try and reproduce the same end result with each client. As the questions asked change, the reality will change. There is no 'formula' to reproduce the same results over and over again.

A trap that many coaches fall into is assuming that the problem presented by the person in front of them is the same as the one presented by a client last week. They then believe that last week's solution will be today's solution (Cooperrider & Whitney; n.d).

4. The Anticipatory Principle

What drives many people and most of the activities in a company is an image of the future. It is a specific expectation of what the company should look like or be able to achieve.

As human beings we are constantly looking towards the future; it influences what we do in the present. It is after all this image of the future that motivates us into action. Positive future outlooks will ultimately lead to positive actions and positive results.

The Placebo effect in medicine is a good example of this. According to the Placebo effect, up to 40% of test subjects receiving only a placebo will experience the same positive results as those test subjects receiving the real medication. Of course there is no scientific reason why this is the case; there is only the anticipation of a positive outcome.

Aristotle is known for saying: "A vivid imagination compels the whole body to obey it." (Cooperrider & Whitney; n.d)

Further food for thought for coaches and therapists of all kinds is that in one experiment, the placebo response increased to 62% when the doctor treated them with "warmth, attention, and confidence." (Kaptchuk et al 2008).

5. The Positive Principle

This principle relies on the positive bond between people and their own positive emotions. Together these not only affect, but also maintain, affirmative change. These include qualities like hope, encouragement, compassion, solidarity, sense of meaningfulness and sheer excitement at the thought of creating something purposeful together.

It is this principle which makes it essential that all questions are asked in an unconditionally positive manner. This strengthens the positive social interaction amongst colleagues (Cooperrider & Whitney; n.d).

Radical Coaching and Appreciative Inquiry know that the aim of the positive question is not to receive an 'acceptable' or 'unacceptable' answer. The purpose is to hear, appreciate, be amazed and enthused by the people who share their realities with us. Expect miracles!

The Cycle of Appreciative Inquiry

Appreciative Inquiry is often described as a cycle of 4 D's, Discovery, Dream, Design and Destiny. These revolve around a core containing the Affirmative Topic chosen for the Appreciative Inquiry process (Cooperrider & Whitney; n.d).

Topic Choice

Most Affirmative Action Programs tend to have between three to five topic choices. Consequently a company or individual may work through three to five cycles to affect positive change. Radical Coaches can help businesses or individuals identify what is truly important to them. They can lead them through the cycle of Appreciative Inquiry towards positive change.

The topic choice is at the core of the cycle because it guides the whole process.

Appreciative Inquiry (AI) and Radical Coaching believe that the questions that are asked are ultimately what lead to change. The questions are seen as the seeds of change, because it is ultimately what causes people to stop and reconsider. Therefore AI says that asking the questions and the change that occurs from these questions indeed happen in the same instant.

It is after all through questions and answers that most discoveries in history have been made and the same rule applies to AI.

Some of the commonly used topics center on words like improvement, commitment, reliability, enablement, environmental responsibility, sense of ownership and pride. A topic may be anything that an individual or company may feel is important, either in a humanitarian or strategic way (Cooperrider & Whitney; n.d).

Radical Coaching acknowledges that companies are driven by human beings. Therefore the system will always move in the direction of the people's most frequently asked questions. The frequency with which these questions are uttered, will also indicate the importance of these questions to the human driven system.

Discovery

The process of discovery requires an extensive inquiry process centered on the chosen affirmative topic. Ideally, discovery needs to include as many of the people involved as possible. Inquiry is what this phase is all about.

One way in which a Radical Coach may achieve this, is to take a handful of people in a company and train them. They need be able to have an appropriate Appreciative Inquiry Interview with as many people as possible within their same company. These interviews in turn revolve around a common positive topic chosen for the specific Appreciative Inquiry Cycle.

There are many advantages to having as many people as possible interview as many people as possible. These advantages include the following:

- Changes are more likely to be effective because as many people as possible are involved in the analysis and decision making processes.

- It creates a better understanding between different role players in an organization.

- It facilities a larger ability for change. People are involved from ground level to the top affecting change in as many areas as possible.

In a way it is the same as studying the atom. Even though the atom is considered to be very small, studies have revealed that it is in fact very powerful. In the same way AI attempts to uncover and reveal every positive aspect of an individual either separately or as part of a company.

This includes every strength, improvement, achievement, available resource, value, hope, passion, etc. In the end this is what determines the company's ultimate potential and developed potential is what leads to success (Cooperrider & Whitney; n.d).

A successful coach knows that it is not just the answers that are important but, as mentioned previously, the questions are what bring about change. The interview is therefore just as important as the information collected from it.

Dream

An artist sits in front of a new canvas and does not see a fault with the white sheet. Instead he or she searches for potential value. In the same way **AI focuses on the potential (what could be),** and not what is wrong with the system or individual.

The next phase of AI involves creating a common dream or a common goal. It requires the ability to be appreciated by many and the strength to inspire all who share that dream.

In a company, all the data collected from the interviews are combined and shared with the involved individuals. The feedback can be given in many ways, sometimes creatively as the 'story' of the company or an individual's life. It may also be given in an interpretive and analytic way.

A good coach will know the best way to share this feedback with his or her clients, either as an individual or the whole company. The manner in which it is presented is however not as important as the fact that it points clearly towards a positive image of the future – the dream.

What probably distinguishes the Radical Coaching and Appreciative Inquiry dream from any other psychological dream is the fact that it is not abstract. It is not a 50/50 dream. It does not have either a 50% chance of coming true or a 50% chance of never becoming a reality.

It is founded in the actual positive past, or even present, of either the individual or the company. It has indeed already happened before and the aim is to make it a permanent, positive future habit as well (Cooperrider & Whitney; n.d).

In the dream stage it is important to determine the ideal environment in which these positive things happened. The aim is then to reproduce this environment on a continuous basis.

'Inspiring Proposals' are future ideals that need to be written down. People need to continuously be reminded about these ideals to keep them motivated. For a proposal to be inspiring it needs to meet the following criteria:

- Does the proposal have the potential to challenge or transform?

- Is it founded in real, past, positive experiences?

- Do the members of the organization share the same passion for the proposal?

- Is it written in bold typing, using positive terminology and in the present tense? (Coaching Leaders Ltd; 2012)

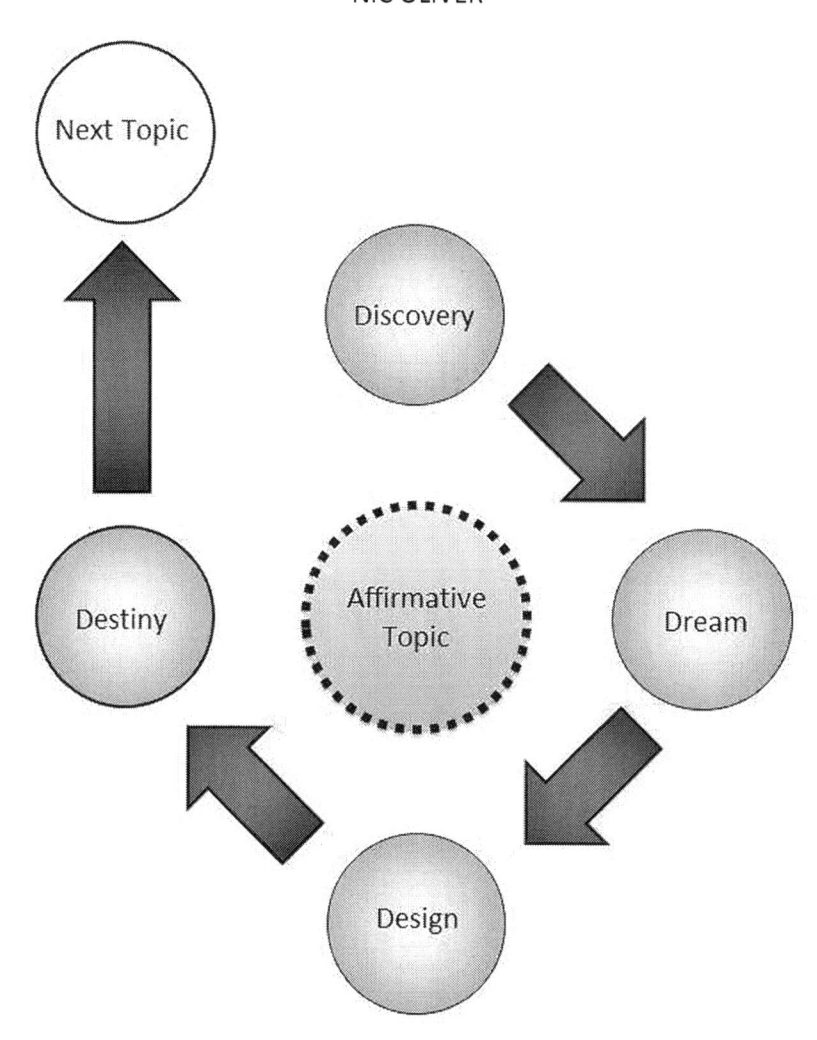

Diagram: A cycle showing "Affirmative Topic" at the center, surrounded by Discovery → Dream → Design → Destiny → Next Topic.

Design

The success of the design phase relies on three things:

1. The image of an enhanced world/life/company.

2. A potent drive.

3. A convincing declaration of deliberate intent.

Another factor which greatly influences the design phase is the success of the dream phase.

It's important with Radical Business Coaching to never neglect the Dream phase. It may appear to be the easiest part of the cycle or the part which requires the least activity. However, it is the dream phase that has the power to unite people and organizations and to focus their attention on a common goal. It's the carrot in front of the horse's nose, the thing that will ultimately convince it to move forward.

The design phase excludes any form of bureaucracy in order to be beneficial. The aim of Radical Business Coaching is to remind people of the fact that they have the power to affect the world around them. In the design phase of AI, all people involved in the situation need to be involved in making decisions. Power should be equally distributed.

It is important that all the people involved agree on a set of design principles. These are not necessarily fixed actions. Instead it describes the attitudes or creed that will influence the way in which people move forward, for example "We believe in gender equality in our workplace." (Cooperrider & Whitney; n.d)

Destiny

William James is known for saying that human beings are the only ones responsible for their own destiny.

Radical Coaching and Appreciative Inquiry are not so much about having a set of fixed rules that deliver a predetermined outcome. The aim of Radical Coaching and AI is to bring about positive changes in the workplace or within individuals. These are based upon change in peoples' attitudes towards each other and the realities which they created through these attitudes.

It is looking at the world around us as if we are seeing it fresh and new. This new look is not due to new knowledge. It is rather about remembering all the dreams and ideals that motivated you to join the company in the first place.

Our perceptions ultimately influence how we view life, people, and organizations. It consequently influences the way we interact with the world we live in.

In a way Appreciative Inquiry should lead to a positive movement, which is an ongoing process, instead of a final, deliverable package.

Radical Coaching does not rely strongly on a measurable or tangible outcome either, but rather the setting in motion of positive change. This is after all what growth is and growth is almost always a positive thing.

Neither Radical Coaching nor Appreciative Inquiry relies on control, but rather the free flow of natural, positive change. Just like a green plant, sprouting from a seed, always knows which way is up through the darkness. An individual and a company will find the 'positive' upwards direction in which to grow.

The destiny phase also brings out the fact that sometimes even small discoveries can have a huge impact. It is when people are willing to embrace even these small changes that progress may happen in leaps and bounds (Cooperrider & Whitney; n.d).

CHAPTER 21: THE POTENTIAL OF APPRECIATIVE INQUIRY IN RADICAL COACHING

"Seek out that particular mental attribute which makes you feel most deeply and vitally alive, along with which comes the inner voice which says, "This is the real me," and when you have found that attitude, follow it." William James

Appreciative Inquiry relies strongly on the viewpoint that nothing is wrong with people or organizations to start with. Sound familiar? This has the potential to lift a large amount of weight off peoples' shoulders. People are not being 'accused' or 'caught out' and placed in the spotlight for everything they have done wrong in their past.

Appreciative Inquiry has the ability to empower people. People make up the organizations and communities they live in, so they can change these social settings for the better (Cooperrider & Whitney; n.d).

When people are united in a common goal the improvements are seen much sooner and have a greater impact. Appreciative Inquiry can unite people and focus their attention on a common goal (Cooperrider & Whitney; n.d).

A frame of reference is always useful as a foundation. Appreciative Inquiry provides people with a true frame of reference from their past. This past frame makes it easier to believe in the future because it is built on something that has happened before (Cooperrider & Whitney; n.d).

Great Questions and Phrases

I've adapted the following list of questions from the book "Appreciative Coaching: A Positive Process for Change." to give you a flavor of how the emphasis of Radical Coaching is very different from most other approaches.

Great Phrases

- "My instinct in this situation is…"
- "I have a hunch that…"
- "The first thing that occurred to me when you said that was…"
- "I don't feel that you are truly connected/committed (whatever) to what you just said."
- "I would like to give you some feedback."

Then describe the client's behavior and its effect. For example:

- "I would like to give you some feedback. You talked about being embarrassed about a guilty secret. I've mentioned it three times and each time you've changed the subject. What's this about?"

- "You didn't turn up to our last session and I was left hanging for 20 minutes. This isn't the first time this is happened and I'm concerned that coaching isn't a priority for you at the moment."

- "Every time we start to discuss 'X', you look down at the table which breaks eye contact. The result is that you lose impact."

Once you have given feedback, be quiet and listen to the client. Be patient and don't fill the silence. So the simple formula is:

- State their behavior (what they did or said or didn't do or say).

- State the effect of the behavior.

- If appropriate, describe your feelings.

- Be quiet and listen.

Other Useful Phrases

- "When you…" e.g. "When you are told you have to give a presentation to the board, what's the first thing that happens for you internally?"

- "You might find that..." e.g. "You might find that, when you have that conversation with her, you are pleasantly surprised by her response."

- "What would it be like if...?" e.g. "What would it be like if you were to try 'X'?"

- "A person can sometimes feel..." e.g. "A person can sometimes feel that their boss is annoyed with them when the boss's frustration has nothing to do with them."

- "I'd like to invite you to notice..." e.g. "I'd like to invite you to notice the first thought that comes to you when I tell you that you are a very powerful person."

- "It's not necessary to..." e.g. "It's not necessary for your product to be perfect before you launch it."

QUICK COMPARISON

	Three Principles	Positive Psychology	Appreciative Inquiry	Radical Coaching
Historical Influences/Founders	William James Sydney Banks Roger Mills George Pransky	Carl Rogers Abraham Maslow Henry Murray Gordon Allport Rollo May Martin Seligman Mihaly Csikszentmihalyi	Stowell West	Founder Nic Oliver Influencers Rich Litvin Steve Chandler Michael Neill Richard Bandler Sydney Banks Christian Mickelsen
Principles	Mind Consciousness Thought	Self-acceptance Growth Incorporation of personality Self-government Perceiving reality accurately Mastering the environment	Constructionist Simultaneity Poetic Anticipatory Positive	If it works, use it. Perception = reality. Only ever work in the client's highest good. Honor the Wisdom that created the client's and coach's beings How can I serve you?

RADICAL COACHING

	Three Principles	Positive Psychology	Appreciative Inquiry	Radical Coaching
Methods	Understanding the power of thoughts Controlling thoughts	**Measuring:** Subjective well-being Strength of Character Engagement & Flow Meaning	**Cycle of 4 D's revolving around an Affirmative Topic:** Discovery Dream Design Destiny	Meaningful conversations Blend 3Ps, PP and AI.
Focus	Thoughts	Emotions	Words	The individual as a whole – thoughts, emotions and words.
Outcome	Creating a better 'reality' through the process of mental activity	Pleasant Life Engaged Life Meaningful Life	Setting in motion of positive change without requiring a fixed outcome	Transforming lives. Helping the best to get even better.

:: PART 2 ::

INTRODUCTION TO PART 2

In Part 2 you will first get the chance to think about you, the coach, what success means to you and what your 'Wow!' life will be. We'll also look at four different kinds of coaching, in case you are unsure of the kind of coach you want to be.

If you work your way through the questions, you'll end up with a lot of quality information that will be important in building your business.

Finally in this part, we will look at different aspects of hosting powerful conversations.

CHAPTER 22: YOUR PERSONAL COACHING MOTIVES

"Follow Your Passion, Find Your Power". Bob Doyle

Before setting up any kind of business, there are two different sets of questions you need to ask yourself. The first set relates to personal motives for being in business for yourself, while the second set asks some basic business questions. Why? Because if you want to succeed, you have to find your business sweet spot, the intersection of your purpose, passion, strengths and the value you can bring others.

You need to understand something fundamental from the outset: In order to succeed in business, you need to be prepared to go against the grain. 80% of small business startups fail to survive and are not thriving after their first five years. To put it another way, there are two kinds of business failure:

1. Crash and Burn, like Borders, Blockbuster videos etc.

2. Zombies - the walking dead, lurching from one bill to another. The business is barely alive and their owners have swapped being a wage slave for being a slave to their business.

The instructive thing is that most of the 80% which don't survive and thrive are all reading the same books, attending the same workshops, receiving the same advice from business coaches!

So, if following the conventional wisdom is a route to failure at least 80% of the time, it makes sense to do something different. Think of the successful Dragon's Den lenders. Or think of Alan Sugar, Donald Trump, Richard Branson, Bill Gates, Steve Jobs etc. They were all mavericks! Doesn't that tell you something?

The 80% who fail, all knew the same stuff, more or less, which leads us to a key principle:

"Your success is determined by how you think, not by what you know!"

Time and again, research reveals that most coaches earn less than $20,000 a year. Do you want to be in that group or do you want a 6 figure annual income? It's your choice!

Question Set 1 - Personal Motivation

1. Defining Success

Ask most people to define success and they restrict their answers to one or two areas of life. We take a holistic approach that encompasses The 8 Pillars of Success. So ask yourself what success means to you in each of the following areas:

1. Family
2. Financial
3. Physical
4. Recreation
5. Relationships
6. Self
7. Spiritual
8. Work

The questions that follow are written in the present tense as they are written assuming that you are leading your 'Wow' life and ask you to describe it!

1. Family

- When you are successful, what will your relationship be like with your family?

- How much time will you spend with them?

- How many holidays a year will you take with them?

2. Financial

- When you are successful, how much money will you have?

- What will you spend it on?

3. Physical

- When you are successful, what will you be doing to take good care of yourself?

4. Recreation

- When you are successful, what hobbies will you be taking part in?

- Who with?

- How often?

5. Relationships

- When you are successful, other than family, which will be your key relationships?

- How involved will you be in your community?

- What will you be doing?

- What will your social life be?

6. Self

- When you are successful, what will you be doing to make sure you keep on learning, to keep on growing?

7. Spiritual

- When you are successful, what will your spiritual life be?

- What spiritual activities will you be embracing?

8. Work

- When you are successful, what work will you continue to do?

- What will be most important to you in your work?

Now, go back to each of the answers you gave and ask yourself two simple questions:

1. What has changed?

2. What did I do to successfully make those changes?

2. Finding your Purpose

Ask yourself the following:

- What is important to me?

- What am I doing when I feel the most inspired, loving and grateful?

- What am I most passionate about?

- What am I really good at?

- What can I do for hours and not notice time passing by?

- If success was guaranteed, what one great thing would I do?

- If I could design my ideal life, what service would I be giving to mankind?

3. Combining Purpose and Passion

Once you have established what your purpose is you need to combine it with your passion. The following exercises are designed to ask you some tough questions but the result will be a clear statement of where you want to be going and why.

First some important questions:

- Why is this a good time for you to find your purpose and to make a commitment to achieving your goals?

- What would happen if you didn't change anything at all?

- What's missing from your life at the moment?

- What is holding you back?

Question Set 2. Your Ideal Work Life

Imagine someone waved a magic wand and you had your 'Wow' life. What would your work and personal lives be like? Answer the next 4 questions in the context of your 'Wow' life.

1. In your 'Wow!' life, what is your ideal work week?

    - Do you have a lazy morning and then work in the afternoon for a few hours?

    - Do you work in the morning and do other things in the afternoon?

- When you do work, how many hours a day do you work?

- What are your main responsibilities?

2. In your 'Wow!' Life, what is your work environment like?

3. In your 'Wow!' life, who do you work with?

4. In your 'Wow!' life, what makes you proud about your work?

CHAPTER 23: RADICAL COACHING MODEL

"The brain is biological whereas the Mind is spiritual." Sydney Banks

Generally speaking, Radical Coaches avoid being constrained by coaching models – the essence of Radical Coaching is to be fully present with your client and deal with whatever comes up.

However, if you want a simple model to guide you, think of four steps:

1. What to change?

2. What to change to?

3. How to change?

4. Measuring change – is the client getting the change(s) he/she wants.

Implications of having 'Clients' rather than 'Customers'

Coaches talk of having 'clients' but most coaches don't realize the importance of the choice of words.

Customers are transaction based – there is no relationship beyond the transaction.

Clients are in a relationship with you under your duty of care – you have a responsibility to always give the best advice; to always act in their highest good. This is why non-directive coaching is both a myth and is, in any case, undesirable. If you withhold your best advice in order to be non-directive, you are falling short on both counts!

What kind of coach do you want to be?

There is certainly good money to be made as a coach; both online and offline (people who invest in coaching are typically committed to success and willing to pay!). But in order to know who needs your services, you need to be aware of the basic facts about coaching in the twenty-first century, as well as what options to choose.

There is no greater joy than helping people achieve goals, break through stubborn barriers and better their quality of life. This chapter will introduce you to four of the most currently popular Coaching Programs, both online and off.

Read through the models and see if one of them resonates with your own life goals. You may not have previously considered coaching... but could one of these be you?

1. Personal (or Life) Coach

A Personal Coach helps clients identify, adjust and create empowering personal goals, with a strong focus on improving quality of life.

Typical areas a Personal Coach might help with include identifying and taking action on:

- Your client's most fulfilling purpose.
- What is holding them back.
- How to remove blockages, take action and move forward.
- How to achieve balance and harmony in their personal life.
- How to maintain their new, dynamic, balanced way of life.

Coaching requires strong listening and facilitating skills. Furthermore, being well-balanced and skilled in maintaining empathy combined with objectivity are also core essentials.

Coaching is not Therapy!

Coaching means hosting meaningful conversations that transform lives by helping people to get what they want.

To most authorities, Therapy means helping people overcome the problems of their past and requires qualifications/licensing.

Requirements:

In some ways, becoming a Personal Coach is one of the easiest areas to break into, because it's largely unregulated. If you want to, you can voluntarily take general accreditation courses with bodies such as the IAC (International Association of Coaches), an organization that attempts to standardize the level of coaching in all disciplines.

Most people find that as they begin their practice, they start to specialize in certain areas. If there are courses relevant to these areas, most Coaches will take them, adding accreditation to their résumés. Some do not.

Some base their work totally on intuition and skills acquired through life experience; some own the credential of many hours' experience and expertise in their chosen field.

Successful, enthusiastic clients are your most important credential! Remember – people pay for results, not for coaching!

Variations:

Some areas currently popular in Personal Coaching:

- Business Coach: Focus on achieving business goals through personal power.

- Personal Coach: Focus on personal goals, blockage removal and balanced wholeness.

- Spiritual Coach: Focus on spiritual energy and harmony, either through traditional religions or more esoteric areas such as Reiki.

- Organization Coach: Focus on helping people overcome lifelong habits of clutter or create efficient work spaces under challenging conditions.

Rewards:

The ability to make the most of your own passions and strengths to help others, makes Personal Coaching one of the most rewarding disciplines. Seeing people go from frustrated and stuck in ruts and patterns to glowing with personal power and succeeding beyond their wildest dreams is something you can't put a price on -- though the more successful you are, the higher the fee you can command.

Earning Base-line:

$500 - $1,000 per month, though many personal coaches earn more.

2. Business Coach

A Business Coach will borrow tools from Personal Coaching, but the focus is more work-oriented, often including such concrete elements as making a focused business plan, handling finances, developing promotional strategies, etc.

A Business Coach, who specializes in online marketing coaching, helps guide newer marketers through all the basic steps of running an online business, often taking them right from the ground level up. This involves scam-proofing and helping them save time and money by avoiding common traps (such as the dreaded 'information overload').

Requirements:

Experience is the most important credential in Business Coaching, as well as a thorough understanding, balanced overview and mastery of all areas of business practice. The more hours you've logged, the more effective you will be.

Again, the ability to specialize allows you to make the most of skills you've honed in the field. You can acquire credentials through courses in various, specific techniques (such as Shadow Coaching™). University Business Degrees also add impact to your profile.

The most important requirement is being even a few steps ahead of your target client base in your own career journey. You need to be able to show them how to do what you're currently succeeding at.

As with any other area of coaching, successful clients become your best testimonial - and a powerful networking tool both for yourself and your newer clients.

Variations:

Some areas currently popular in Business Coaching:

- Executive Coach: Focus on helping clients to walk the executive path in a manner that gets measurable results and inspires personal and professional respect.

- Career Coach: Focus on helping clients to find their true career path and attain it.

- Leadership Coach: Focus on helping clients become a strong leader in team situations.

- Time Management Coach: Focus on helping clients to stay organized and manage time efficiently in order to achieve more and make money.

Rewards:

Seeing people become proactive leaders and start earning their full potential, with confidence and power, is the biggest reward this profession can bring.

Earning Base-Line:

$500 - $1,500 per month, though many business coaches earn more.

3. Family Coach

A Family Coach helps families become positive, effective units, producing healthy children and wise parents with a close, team-oriented, marital relationship. Some coaches focus on specific issues or problems; others on general personal self-development for all family members.

Requirements:

Family coaching is based on experience but often leans a little more heavily on certification than other types of coaching. There are many specific methods or areas one can acquire training and certification in. You can also obtain training and general certification with schools such as PCI (Parent Coaching Institute).

If you want to specialize in helping people deal with specific challenges that require a deep understanding (such as ADHD or Autism), training and certification in these specific areas is strongly recommended and will increase your perceived value in the eyes of your target clientele.

Variations:

- Teen Parenting Coach: Focus on helping teens integrate happily with the rest of the household or on overcoming specific problems such as behavioral issues, failure at school, depression, etc.

- Special Needs Coach: Focus on household coping with the additional challenges of special needs children, including Autism, ADHD, Downs Syndrome, Mobility challenges, etc.

- Divorce Parenting Coach: often working closely with the judicial system, this type of coach focuses on helping children and parents undergoing separation scenarios create the healthiest 'new normal'.

- Baby Coach: Focus on guiding new mothers through the first years of their infants' lives, often beginning as early as actual pregnancy and birth onwards to kindergarten and junior school.

Rewards:

Seeing families become strong, positive units while problems recede and new, healthier patterns are created.

Knowing parents are enjoying their children or finding relief and support in dealing with special challenges.

Earning Base Line:

$500+ per month, with many family coaches earning much more.

4. Fitness Coach

When people talk of Fitness Coaches, the old assumption used to be 'Personal Trainer', with the latter riding hard on a sweating client at the local gym.

Nowadays, a fitness coach can operate successfully online, helping people conquer lifestyle issues such as weight loss or dealing with health challenges.

Requirements:

Experience can often outweigh credentials in this area of coaching. For example, with weight loss, having lost weight and kept it off is probably the most powerful credential! In other areas, appropriate certification certainly adds perceived and real value to your services. If you are going to deal with issues such as creating a healthy diet, for example, a background as an accredited nutritionist or dietitian is a definite plus - both for you and your client.

Variations:

1. Wellness Coach: Focus on optimizing and increasing general mental and physical health.

2. Urban Fitness Coach: Focus on helping people circumnavigate the dangers of urban and sedentary lifestyles.

3. Weight Loss Coach: Focus on helping people permanently lose weight and develop new, healthier patterns of maintaining the ideal weight.

4. Sports/Fitness Coach: Focus is usually on specific sports, as well as on broader issues such as avoiding injury, dealing with physiological challenges, pacing oneself for maximum performance or simply maintaining a healthy lifestyle that includes exercise.

Rewards:

Seeing people enjoy the benefits of better health, life expectancy, maximum performance, increased confidence and stronger physical energy.

Earning Base Line:

$500+ per month, with many fitness coaches earning much more.

CHAPTER 24: THE COACHING LADDER

"It's essential (especially in today's economy) to be positioned as an Expert." Daniel Wagner

I have listed just four different coaching areas and there are many more. What's important is that you choose an area that you are passionate about and set about establishing yourself as an expert. What follows is a summary of a model created by Daniel Wagner (2013). I strongly recommend that you read his book and put what he writes into practice (always the tough bit!).

The First Rung – The Generalist Coach

Generalist coaches earn very little because the market is saturated with them – research consistently shows that such coaches earn less than $20,000 a year.

The Second Rung – The Specialist Coach

There are fewer coaches on this rung so, in accordance with the Law of Supply and Demand, these coaches earn more money. They will specialize in a niche but are often constrained by a finite number of hours in the week.

The Third Rung – The Expert Coach

It used to be extremely difficult to position yourself as an expert and to provide leadership to a niche. A lot of money or time or both were needed. Now, the internet has leveled the playing field.

Interestingly, being acknowledged as an expert is largely a matter of perception; all that is required is that your niche market perceives you as an expert.

Experts can pick and choose how many clients they have – Rich Litvin only has 5 clients at a time! Experts are very selective about who has direct access to them.

Some Experts have multiple streams of income with offerings at different price points. The commonly used phrase is a "Strategic Sales Funnel." At the wide end are cheap products that sell in high volume. As you move through the funnel, there are a number of products that are increasingly expensive and sell to fewer people.

There are very few coaches operating at this level and those that are frequently bring in high 6 or even 7 figure annual incomes.

The Top Rung – The Celebrity Coach

Less than 1% reach this level – think Anthony Robbins, Paul McKenna or Dr. Phil for example. At this level, you can sell pretty much anything based on your name alone!

Which brings with it a responsibility – people will try to use your name to imply endorsements that you know nothing about!

By the way, you can leverage Celebrity names as long as it's legitimate. I learned this when I told someone that I'd learned NLP from the same person who had taught Anthony Robbins. I was initially surprised at how it had impressed the person I was speaking with.

It was only later that I thought about how you can benefit from being associated with such celebrities.

CHAPTER 25: THE ART OF GREAT CONVERSATIONS

"Hear what they want to hear and disregard the rest."
Simon and Garfunkel

The quote reflects the way many people approach conversations. However, whichever of the approaches described in Part 3 you take to building your business, coaching is about hosting powerful conversations; conversations that have the ability to transform your clients' lives.

In order to achieve this, you need to first possess great conversational skills and this is what this chapter is all about.

Take this information and apply it to both your social life as well as your practice. In the end it is about you being authentic, being real and the first way of achieving this is to 'practice what you preach.'

Why is having a great conversation important?

Human beings are social beings; we like to communicate our ideas, our thoughts and emotions and we use conversation as the main means of communication. All types of coaching rely heavily on conversational communication, but doing it right is more important than just talking.

Conversation fundamentals

Most of us can spot a phony smile or an insincere compliment and it is the same with a forced conversation. Conversations should be comfortable, natural and above all genuine.

I know there's a risk of teaching you to suck eggs but for sake of completeness, let's review the important fundamentals of quality conversations:

Smile: This way you will come across as being friendly and warm. If a client has to pick between a friendly coach with a smile and an aloof one with a frown, which one do you think they will choose?

Make eye contact: Eye contact should be friendly, breaking your gaze every now and then to prevent yourself from staring at people. At this point it is important to mention the need to avoid looking away while discussing important topics. It may seem as if you are being dishonest. Your clients will share many personal aspects of their lives with you and they need to know that you can be trusted with the information.

Project friendliness: It may be as simple as relaxing your arms at your sides, instead of folding them across your chest.

Don't try too hard: You do not want to be perceived as being desperate or too dependent on your client's money.

These are just the basic things to remember when you are planning on starting a conversation with a new client.

They may seem obvious but I've learned to check myself regularly and to ask for feedback from clients and friends. In spite of over 30 years of experience as a coach, I recently discovered that when I was thinking about what a client has said, I was breaking eye contact and looking down to my left.

This can give totally the wrong message to clients, especially to those who place high value in eye contact.

Value

When people approach you for coaching it is because they believe that you have some knowledge or ability, which they don't have, and which can help them improve their lives.

The value of coaching conversations often relies on a simple thing: the power of being listened to. How often have you had someone focus just on you and listen to you without interruption, without judgment and totally for your benefit? Many people never benefit from such a conversation – until they meet you!

Add in the power of meaningful questions and your coaching conversations will provide extremely high value to your clients.

Contribute value – Meaningful questions

I've already mentioned this before, but one of my favorite ways to begin the first coaching session is to ask:

"Imagine we are sitting here, having this conversation, 3 years from now and you are living your 'Wow" life. Thinking back over those 3 years, what must have happened to you, in both your professional and personal lives, for you to feel good about your progress?"

Use the power of the pause – in other words, give the client time to process the question, to imagine their "Wow" life and what must have happened in the interim.

Be patient – give them the opportunity to respond. When the time is ready, you can be more specific by asking:

- "What five strengths did you leverage?"
- "What five weaknesses have you addressed?"
- "What five opportunities did you seize?"
- "What five problems have you had to overcome?"

Asking them to prioritize the four lists and the answers to the above will give you enough material to be coaching for months, and it will be tailored to each client! What more can a client ask for?

At any stage in this process, whether the original question or the follow-up SWOP, you can ask "What's important to you about that?" until you have dug down and found the core issues.

For example, in answering the original question, they may say "I drive a big people carrier." There could be several reasons for this: status, to go off road, to go camping etc. By asking "What's important to you about that?" you'll find their reason. In this case, "So all of the family can fit in, the kids can bring their bikes and toys and we can all get away for weekend breaks together." You've now got a lot of important information!

With existing clients who will have already answered the above, a question Rich Litvin often asks is useful: "How can I best serve you in this moment?" Again, in most cases, whatever they answer can be followed up with "What's important to you about that?"

Help them to SOAR

Alternatively, you can use the SOAR model from AI which can be used with individuals and organizations. I've written a brief overview of the model. More detail can be found in Stavros and Hinrichs (2009).

The letters stand for:

Strengths

Opportunities

Aspirations

Results

The model helps people to:

- Identify and leverage strengths.
- Identify and seize opportunities.
- Clarify their aspirations, vision and major purpose.
- Align their goals with each other so that there is no inner conflict.
- Decide on the results they are seeking.
- Create strategies and plans for achieving those results in a way that is consistent with their aspirations, vision and major purpose.

Don't try and add all the value

As a coach, you may be holding all the cards with regard to education and experience. It is the client, however, who needs to reveal the areas in which these skills may be useful or not. The client's input in a conversation is more important than the coach's. A shovel is useless if it has no ground to work in and the same applies to the conversation between a coach and a client.

You may also come across as a people pleaser if you are constantly providing the 'entertainment.' What's more, you and the other person will remain strangers to each other and you won't be able to earn your client's trust.

Status

We are all aware of the impact of rank; the higher your rank in society the greater your influence. The danger during a coaching conversation is that the client will put you on a pedestal as 'the problem solver.' Unfortunately, there are some coaches who revel in this. If you are one of them, you have to let go of this tendency both for you and your clients' benefits.

There is another danger, rarely mentioned on coaching courses. As the client starts to experience personal transformation through the powerful coaching conversations that you host, they may come to associate you with the great feelings they have during the conversations. This may lead to their transferring their feelings onto you in the form of strong attachment. Be careful of this, or you can get into situations you hadn't anticipated or sought!

Embracing servant leadership will help you to avoid this because it will lead to you taking a 'lower' position in a conversation, which will benefit your client, and consequently yourself, over the long term.

Constant flow of thoughts

As discussed earlier in this book our minds are continuously being flooded with new thoughts and new ideas.

To have a great conversation, you need to know how to pick the thoughts that are relevant to the phase of the conversation you are in. Usually your mind will respond to the situation you are currently in and present you with relevant thoughts anyway. Acquire the skill to distinguish the most useful thoughts from the less useful ones and build the former into your conversations.

As a coach you will eventually learn how to use your own as well as your clients' flow of thoughts to lead them into the right direction, to reveal their core issues. If you notice that a client is not yet ready to open up to you, rather lead the conversation into safer emotional territory. Focus on building a relationship of trust first.

Connection

The whole purpose behind conversation is to build relationships. Relationships are what keep families and societies together and ultimately it is what will keep your clients coming back for more necessary sessions.

People who are in a relationship experience some sort of connection with another human being and it is this connection that binds them together. This connection is dependent on certain emotional experiences, specifically the experience of comfort and trust.

It is when people trust you and feel comfortable in your presence that you build a connection with them.

This is really very important in any conversation and especially in a coaching conversation. So how do you get them to trust you and feel comfortable around you?

Be genuine

It really can't be emphasized enough: Be genuine. Be real. We have all heard the saying "what you see is what you get".

Too many coaches try to be someone else – Anthony Robbins, Dr. Phil, etc. Be yourself – there's nobody else you can be!

People can immediately see if you are faking it through either your body language, the tone in your voice and any other non-verbal cue you may give them. This really has some serious implications that you need to consider.

Do you really want to have meaningful, great, powerful, transformational coaching conversations with people? This is probably the most important question coaches need to ask themselves. The answer will determine how real you are when talking to people. If you like your dog more than the lady sitting in front of you, it will show. You will probably not end up having a satisfactory relationship.

This implies that in order for you to have great conversations with people, it's not enough to *like* people. You need to passionately *love* people and be intrigued by them before you will be able to engage in great life altering conversations.

If you do not feel this strong affection for people it will show up in your voice, your body language, your gaze, the amount of effort you are willing to put in the conversation, etc. People will catch onto this emotional coldness and just walk out of your life. No conversation there and consequently no relationship.

Using questions correctly

How often you ask questions can either contribute to the natural flow of a coaching conversation or kill it in an instant.

A coaching conversation is not an interview! Remember the last time you went for a work interview. You were probably feeling a bit nervous and couldn't wait for it to be over. Well, why recreate this same atmosphere by continuously placing someone else in the hot seat? Will you really be surprised if all they want to do is get up and run?

Many coaches fall into a simple trap; we are so eager to get to the heart of the problem that we literally interrogate our clients. Until we know what is 'wrong' with them we are too afraid to contribute some information ourselves. As we've seen, in Radical Coaching, this problem is less likely to occur as we don't believe that anything is 'wrong' with our clients.

They may forget the good things that have happened to them. They may overlook their strengths. Most of all, they may be guilty of faulty thinking. But there's nothing 'wrong' with them. They don't need fixing!

Setting boundaries

Just like boundaries are necessary for good relationships, they are also necessary for great conversations, and coaching conversations are no different.

How does this apply to coaching? Many people like being the 'victim' of life and circumstances, blaming everyone and everything other than themselves for all of their disappointments. They will attend one coaching session after the other, but never seem to be making any progress. The attention they are getting is enough to pacify the negative emotions they experience, at least until their next session. They have no intention of finding a permanent solution.

This is not only bad for them, but also for you as a coach. Can you imagine a more frustrating scenario than seeing the same client for the thousandth time, having gone around in circles, trying every trick in the book and still not seeing any progress? It will definitely not be good for your self-esteem as a coach or for your track record...

How do you draw boundaries during conversations?

Use the principle of reinforcement. Behavior that you reinforce will ultimately become the way people behave towards you. If you reinforce positive behavior, that type of behavior will be displayed towards you. If you reinforce negative behavior that will become the normal way people will behave towards you.

You will need to be able to control your inner emotions so that your outer actions will reflect the inner calm you are experiencing.

So if a client is taking their temper out on you, using you as a punching bag, try to remain emotionally calm. In the end you will not only be protecting yourself from future negative behavior. You will also help the other person overcome the negative habits they have formed, once they see it is not effective anymore.

CHAPTER 26: THE INITIAL COACHING CONVERSATION

"How can you give them an experience they'll remember for the rest of their lives?" Rich Litvin

So, you've answered all of the questions, done some marketing and are now facing your first client – Now what? I am not going to give you a script – the words that sound right for you won't sound right for me and vice versa.

What I've set out below are the different stages you may go through in a typical Radical Coaching Initial coaching session:

- Connect – "Tell me a little bit about 'x'" (Where 'x' is what they want to talk about). i.e. "Tell me a little bit about your business."

- Engage – Discussion about 'x' – coach asks questions and listens.

Share – Show your vulnerability. Show you are human too! If you've experienced something similar to the topic you are discussing with your client and made a mistake or made a fool of yourself, admit it! I've mentioned this before, but please, **please, please** avoid saying "I understand how you feel." I know many coach training companies tell you to say this but they're wrong! We can never fully understand the other person's feelings, because no matter how similar the circumstances everyone has a different model of the world.

- Trust – the aim of the first 3 steps is to build trust; you may have to go round the first 3 steps several times.

- Dream – people hire coaches to help them achieve their dreams. So a great place to start is with a question like: "Imagine you are now living your 'Wow' life – what would be happening in your personal and professional lives?"

- Impact – This need be no more than to ask them: "What's important to you about...?" or "What would having 'x' do for you?"

- Presentation for Coaching – Chris Mickelsen recommends that you ask one very powerful, magical question. Say: "I have a coaching program that's designed specifically to help people overcome these sorts of challenges and achieve these sorts of goals. Would you like to hear a little bit about it?"

There are so many ways you can handle this depending on your personal preference. If it works, use it, as long as it's consistent with the philosophy discussed in Part 1 of the book!

CHAPTER 27: VALUES

"What's important to you about...?" (My favorite coaching question)

I have mentioned several times the value of the question: "What's important to you about...?" If you ask the question several times in succession, you will begin eliciting the client's values.

Be very careful when you do this – the client will be very vulnerable and open to influence at this stage. Indeed, unscrupulous people abuse this when they wish to manipulate somebody. It's that powerful. It's therefore important for Radical Coaches to understand values and how to work safely with clients' values.

What are Values?

- Values are abstract concepts.
- They are our criteria for determining 'right' from 'wrong'.

- They determine how we spend our time.
- They motivate us.
- They may differ in different contexts.
- They are related to beliefs.
- We each have a hierarchy of values with some being more important than others.

How to Discover Values

- As we've already seen, "What's important about...?" is a great starting point in eliciting values. Keep repeating the question until you get an abstract value: "What's important about <answer>?"
- Then ask: "What else is important?" to get the values they are less consciously aware of (often among the most important).

Hierarchy of Values

- Pick two of the values and ask: "If you could only have one of these values, which one would you have?"
- Keep doing this until you have the values ranked in a hierarchical sequence.
- Rewrite the list of values in the order of importance - you may find that some of the values in the list are the same and have merged.

Check for Clashes

For each value, check that it 'goes with' each other value and that they can co-exist peacefully.

CHAPTER 28: POWERFUL GOALS

"People perform better when they are committed to achieving certain goals." Gary Latham

Most coaches learn, or at least know, about the GROW model for goal setting. Here's a different one you can use when GROW may not cover what you want, or when you just fancy a change!

P - Positive

Always set goals using positive language, describing what the client wants, not what they don't want.

O - Own it

- "What can you do to make this happen?"
- "How can you influence the outcome?"
- "What do you need to do to achieve this goal?"

W – What and When

1. "What's your deadline for achieving this?"

2. "Imagine having achieved your goal. What do you see/hear/feel when you have it?"

E – Ecology (Effects on every area of your life)

This is a check of the impact the goal will have on all areas of your life.

1. (a) "What will be happening when you achieve the goal?"

    (b) "What won't be happening when you achieve the goal?"

    (c) "Are there any negative consequences to achieving it?"

2. (a) "How would achieving your goal affect each area of your life?"

    (b) "Who else would be affected by you achieving your goal?"

    (c) "How would achieving your goal affect other people/the planet?"

3. Congruence check:

    (a) "How do you feel about achieving this goal?"

    (b) "Are you 100% committed to achieving your goal?"

(c) "How enthusiastic are you about achieving this goal?", "Do you get a buzz when you think about it?", "If not, adjust the goal until you feel enthusiastic about achieving it!"

R – Resources and Route

1. What resources do you already have that will help you to achieve your goal? What further resources do you need?

2. Reverse engineer your goal. In other words, imagine that we are having this conversation once you have achieved your goal.

3. What must have happened in order for you to have achieved it? And what had to be in place before that? What strengths did you leverage, weaknesses did you address, opportunities did you seize and problems did you overcome?

:: PART 3 ::

INTRODUCTION TO PART 3

In Part 3, I'm going to look at two different approaches to setting up a coaching business.

1. Viewing your business through the PRISM model I developed:

    P: Process Optimization - Making the most of what you already have and do.

    R: Rationale - Internal Rationale: Your Reason for being in business and your mindset. External Rationale: Being perceived as an authority, as the go to person in your niche.

    I: Innovative Offerings.

    S: Selling - Getting people to buy from you through relationship-based sales and marketing.

    M: Mindset - Programming your belief system for success.

2. The 'Prosperous Coach' approach

The brainchild of Rich Litvin and Steve Chandler, this approach rejects the conventional approach. Instead, it focuses on just having two types of conversations – those with potential clients and those with existing clients.

I will only give you a brief taster of the 'Prosperous Coach' approach. Instead, I recommend that you buy the book (details in the bibliography).

As with many things, I think there's an element of truth in both approaches. My natural inclination is towards the 'Prosperous Coach' approach. However, I think it's prudent to have multiple streams of income for those times when the coach can't or doesn't want to work (i.e. on holiday with the family). In this kind of situation, having streams of passive income makes sense to me.

Whichever approach you are drawn to, before we get down to the business of building a coaching business, we need to look at you, the coach!

CHAPTER 29: THE CONVENTIONAL APPROACH TO MARKETING

"The aim of marketing is to make selling redundant." Peter Drucker

Six Key Questions

Take your time with these as these are the most important questions in this section!

1. What is your market?

   - Who are your competitors?

- Have you researched them?

- How will people find out about you and your offering?

- How will you approach them?

2. What is your niche? (your market segment)

    - Where do you want to focus?

    - Which parts of the market are you best equipped to address?

    - Is it profitable? You may want to sell to one armed, left-handed, web-footed window cleaners but you're unlikely to make it profitable!

3. Where are your potential customers located?

    - Online or offline?

    - In a restricted geographical area, worldwide or somewhere in between?

    - How are you going to access them to market to them?

4. What are their needs, wants, expectations and what do they value?

Research, research and then, research! A common mistake lies in making assumptions.

5. What is your offering?

- Is it a single product/service or a range of them?

- Are they stand alone or do you have a sales funnel? (Sales funnel means that you acquire clients by selling them something cheap and then have progressively more expensive products and services that you try to upsell to them).

- What are you good at - what are you best skills?

6. How does your offering address your potential clients' needs, wants, expectations and what they value in a way that is different from your competition's offerings?

Or to put it another way, why should they buy from you rather than from your competitor, Chris Smith.

The Marketing Pitchfork

A simple model for building a strong, sustainable coaching practice is to think of a four pronged pitchfork. The cost at each prong increases, with the 4th being the most costly to the client.

1. Create high quality, high value free content.

2. A continuity site (membership site) or monthly paid for newsletter.

3. Create your main, paid-for product. High quality content in your specialist field.

4. 1 to 1 coaching/mentoring.

CHAPTER 30: BUILDING YOUR RADICAL COACHING BUSINESS – YOUR BUSINESS PRISM

"Most people jump right in and start doing business, and never consider for even a moment that they should have designed their business first." Rich Schefren

This chapter gives you an overview of the PRISM model. The PRISM digital course is currently being created which will go into this material in far more detail and readers of this book will get a discount when the course is launched.

The PRISM Model has been created to distill the work of two people:

1. Jay Abraham. The leading marketing guru who has for a long time talked about the philosophy of pre-eminence, establishing yourself as the go-to expert in your niche.

2. Peter Drucker who wrote that businesses have only two investments they can make: innovation and marketing. Everything else is a cost.

In over 20 years as a business coach I have discovered the following:

- Only 5% of small businesses are thriving after 10 years of existence.

- Small business owners read the same books, attend the same workshops etc.

Therefore, if you do what everyone else is doing, you are pretty much guaranteed to fail.

Most people over-complicate business.

To further develop the PRISM outline introduced on page 209, why a PRISM? Because in optics, a prism breaks down light into its constituent colors. Similarly, your business PRISM will break down your business into its constituent elements!

P: Process Optimization - making the most of what you already have and do. There is no point in trying to build a business on a weak foundation. Furthermore, in strengthening the foundations, you will discover untapped profits!

R: Rationale

- Internal Rationale: Your Reason for being in business and your mindset. Why did you get into business? Do you see yourself as a business owner or as an entrepreneur? What are your beliefs about yourself and money and about being successful?

- External Rationale: Being perceived as an authority, as the go to person in your niche. How do people know you're an expert? What's your story?

I: Innovative Offerings - Why should people buy from you? How are you better than the competition and in what, measurable, way?

S: Selling - Educating the market about your existence and expertise by pull or attraction marketing. The importance of CEST, of building relationships through adding value.

M: Mindset - Making sure that your belief system doesn't undermine your success.

In any coaching business, there are two outputs you are looking for:

1. Get clients.

2. Work with clients.

By the way, for anyone wanting to specialize in business coaching, PRISM and the two outputs apply to any business in any niche.

Whatever kind of coach you are, there's one thing that's important to understand: you are not billing your clients for your time. You are billing them for the new future you are helping them to create.

A useful analogy is to think of cars – if their current lives are on the level of a Fiat 500, their default future will be a Fiat 500. However, with your help, their future could change to become a

Range Rover or an Aston Martin DB9! That's what your clients are paying you for!

Marketing

- Which market are you focusing on?
- What are their needs/wants/expectations and values?
- Where do people in your market hang out?
- What is your offering?
- What problem(s) does it solve? What are its inherent benefits?
- How does your offering meet your market's needs/wants/ expectations/values better than your competition's offerings?

Innovative Offerings

This could fill a whole book on its own – the question you are seeking to answer is how your offerings are better than your competitors, so that you stand out? Done properly, this will reinforce your authority, so there's a double win for you!

The first thing is to revisit the first two questions from the marketing section:

1. Which market are you focusing on?
2. What are their needs/wants/expectations and values?

The challenge is to find an opening to your coaching conversations that will work regardless of people's needs/wants/
expectations and values!

As a starting point, it's a given that most people want to feel good. Most also want to grow – even the best want to get better!

You can easily set yourself above the Generalist Coaches and many specialists if you offer a structured first session, for free, that is built around a simple concept.

Several years ago, I realized that there were two different ways of getting people to think about growth and change so as to build the future they desire:

1. The first is to ask: "What do you need to do to achieve your goals for the next 3 years?"

2. The second is to ask: "Imagine we're 3 years into the future. What has happened in order for you to have achieved your goals?"

I found that invariably, the second form gets more profound answers; presumably because it's hypothetical (you're obviously not 3 years in the future!).

A few years after discovering the above, I did the NLP Practitioner and Master Practitioner courses. I was extremely fortunate to have learnt under Richard Bandler, Paul McKenna and Michael Breen, who were a very well-integrated team, with complementary strengths. The courses caused me to think again about the two different ways of presenting the future, outlined above.

The outcome of the learning was to develop the following question, which I've mentioned previously but is so important that it bears repeating:

"Imagine we were sitting here having this conversation 3 years from now and you were living your 'Wow' life. Thinking back over those 3 years, what must have happened to you, in both your professional and personal lives, for you to feel good about your progress?"

The timescale you set depends on the context and the topic the client wants to work on. I used to use a 5 year time frame but with the rate of change today plus the uncertainty caused by the economic situation, 5 years is too far away for a lot of people or businesses.

In some situations, 30 days might be enough. If you have any doubt, ask your client what timescale they think is appropriate and realistic.

You can make the question and ensuing conversation even more powerful, by using the SWOP analysis described earlier.

The SWOP questions makes it clear that your coaching is all about them and it won't be the kind of question most people will have heard from coaches.

It also makes it clear that you are motivated by wanting to help them, to be of service and not motivated by desperation to get clients!

Incidentally, you don't need to place this in the future. I recently worked with a client who found it extremely difficult to place herself 3 years in the future. My wife, who was working with me, asked the following question, which immediately energized the client "Imagine someone waved a magic wand and you had your Wow life now. What would your work and personal lives be like?"

Bear in mind that everything I have mentioned in this chapter relies upon your having the right mindset – towards money, towards being in business and towards each of the eight spokes on the success wheel. You can never succeed for any length of time without the right mindset.

CHAPTER 31: PRISM SHORTLIST

1. Select your Market and Niche

- What are their needs/wants/expectations/values? This will affect how you market your offering (see point 6).

- What is your offering?

- What problem does your offering solve for them?

- How does your offering differ from your competition's?

2. Name & Brand your Business

- Either include your own name or something catchy – or both!

- Register a domain name that has your name in it. I had to buy nic-oliver.com to start with as nicoliver.com was taken. I have been able to buy the latter since.

3. Create your Website

- Provide something high quality for FREE (report, video, etc.) so people will opt-in to your mailing list.

- Link the free offer to something that is paid for. Alternatively, link it to a high quality free session offer.

4. Decide how you will build your list

- Webinars or podcasts - can be your own content or interviewing others in your niche. You will need to drive traffic to these events through social media marketing.

- Social Media Marketing – my favorite is to use Facebook advertising but you can also consider:

    a. The mailing list you are building from your website

    b. Twitter

    c. LinkedIn

    d. Online Forums but be careful not to spam. It's best to talk about an article you have written and to link to it. In that article will be a mention of your event.

    e. With Joint Venture partners.

5. Advertising

- Online

    a. Pay-per-click. I have to confess that I have never used it. Many people have lost a lot of money using Pay-Per-Click (PPC). If you want to try it, contact my friend the Kenster at 6 Figure Alliance. He's an expert in PPC.

    b. Write articles for sites such as E-zines, send out newsletters, and write blog articles for your own site or guest blogs for other people's sites

    c. Write press releases and submit to relevant sites (outsource this if possible).

- Offline

    a. Networking Events in your niche

    b. Guest speaking at conferences, meetings etc.

6. Marketing strategy – choose between the following:

- Marketing is results focused – content is results focused.

- Marketing is results focused – content is results focused plus contains material focusing on personal and/or spiritual growth.

- Marketing contains some personal/spiritual growth benefits – content is based on personal and/or spiritual growth.

CHAPTER 32: STRATEGIC OFFERING FUNNEL

"A range of strategically sequenced products or services that you offer for purchase at increasing price points." Daniel Wagner

You need to create a strategic offering funnel that goes from high volume/low price offering(s) to low volume/high price offering(s).

For example:

- E-book at $9.00

- Membership site at $39 a month

- Audio course for $99

- Digital course at $199

- Deluxe digital course (with videos etc.) $999

- Group coaching for 10 people at, for example $200 per person per month.

- Personal coaching at $500 per month.

People often forget the power of e-mail as a sales tool, partly because we all get fed-up with being spammed so much! However, a properly setup auto-responder sequence can be a powerful tool. The key is that you are sending four valuable e-mails, all featuring high quality content before trying to sell anything.

CHAPTER 33: THE DANGERS OF FREE SESSIONS

"(Free sessions) are the cornerstone I would say – of long-term, highly successful coaching." Christian Mickelsen

Many coaches offer free sessions without knowing why and/or what they're trying to achieve. They bumble through it, saying things like: "It's to check if we can work together and if there's a fit between us" or something similar.

A variation of this is to "Let's meet for lunch for a chat." If it takes you 30 minutes to drive to the restaurant, an hour's lunch and 30 minutes back ask yourself this. How powerful a coaching session could you have given them on the phone, on Skype, or at your office, in that same two hours?

I know, because I used to do it until I knew better! I remember spending an hour at least with every new client, giving them a free session over a cup of coffee, with no structure and no outcome in mind! It was little more than a cozy 'coaching and cappuccino' chat.

Few of the people I took through a free session became fee-paying clients and I became very skeptical of the free taster session model.

Two people have changed my mind; two very successful coaches who I respect hugely: Rich Litvin and Christian Mickelsen. The latter developed a program called "Free Sessions That Sell" in which he sets out a 3 step model for free coaching sessions (in this case for building a coaching business).

Tell the potential client that the purpose of the free session is to:

1. Create a crystal clear vision for ultimate success in your business.

2. Uncover the hidden challenges that are keeping you from getting all the clients that you want and more.

3. You'll leave the session renewed, reenergized and inspired to create the business of your dreams.

This model can be adapted to provide a free session for any kind of coaching.

As soon as you sit down with them and have broken the ice, you can follow on with the "Wow" question and the SWOP extension.

CHAPTER 34: SALES PROCESS

"In any sales process, it's far more important to stay close to your potential and existing clients than it is to remember fancy sales techniques." Extract from a sales training course I wrote for a client.

When I used to run sales training courses, I used to quote a research report from Hewlett Packard.

They interviewed the CEOs and their deputies in the Top 500 companies and asked them what would lead them to abort a sales meeting. By far the most common reply was if a sales person openly used sales techniques rather than treating the meeting as a human conversation. This should act as a warning to anyone trying to sell anything!

Let's look at a simple e-mail sales process. The key point here is to send a high number of 'content only' e-mails to a low number of sales e-mails.

- **Step 1** – Customer 'signs up' for report via squeeze page on website.

- **Step 2** – Initial email with report download details (same day).

- **Step 3** – Email, inviting the customer to get involved in the 'conversation' by pointing them to the blog and suggesting reader comments (2 days later).

- **Step 4** – Email with unexpected bonus information - something like a 'hidden chapter' is always a customer-winner as you are over-delivering (2 days later).

- **Step 5** – Email about more bonus information, perhaps in another medium such as video or audio. Again it also makes sense to keep the customer/reader up-to-date on the conversation at the blog and again invite them to join in (2 days).

- **Step 6** – Email customer with 'special offer for readers' with some form of discount or special bonus. One-time-only offers work really well, in other words they must act quickly to get the 'deal' (2 days).

- **Step 7** – Customer buys product/service.

CHAPTER 35: THE 'PROSPEROUS COACH' METHOD

Rich Litvin and Steve Chandler (2013) use a completely different approach.

I love the book – it's the best I have ever read on building a coaching practice. But be prepared for a shock!

A quick extract from the site that promotes the book reveals the following:

"Do you want to coach or learn internet marketing?"

"How many times have you heard that you need to "get the word out" in order to get clients? Or that you need a website and a Facebook page and a Twitter account and an email marketing list and business cards, and..."

"Stop. Just stop. Because you don't need any of that!"

Instead, they want you to build your practice one great relationship at a time.

I'm not going to spoil the fun – if you are attracted to this approach, buy the book - and tell the authors I recommended their book to you!

EPILOGUE

It is the curse of being an author, to be continually thinking "I should expand on this, I should add that etc." Eventually, to overcome this paralysis by analysis, I had to say "OK, let's go with what we've got – I can always write another book!"

Oliver Wendell Holmes once said "Most people go to their graves at with their music still in them."

In other words, we (coaches and clients) are all victims of our own invented limits. And this is just as true of our businesses as it is of our personal lives.

I hope that this book has helped you in some way to expand your horizon, demolish your perceived limits and shown you how to begin to build a stronger business. If you need further help, contact me at nic@nic-oliver.com or come to the website at www.nicoliver.com where you will find lots of products, some free downloads and a blog.

By the time you read this book, the Radical Coaching Academy should be open at http://radicalcoachingacademy.com/ with details of training courses, seminars etc.

Thanks for reading.

Nic Oliver

The Radical Coach

ANNEX - THE FEARS THAT HOLD US BACK

It may seem a little strange to talk about the fears and blockages that prevent us from living our dream, but there is a reason. As we examine some of these obstacles, some people find it illuminating; perhaps understanding for the first time why they can't get the results they are seeking. Others gain comfort when they realize that they are not alone in experiencing these constraints on their growth. Here then, in no particular order, is a list of the top ten fears and blockages that people suffer from and that prevent them from achieving and living their dream:

1. Fear of Failure

Do you hold yourself back from doing what you really want to do because you're afraid of failing? If so, ask yourself a simple question – how do you know you will fail? If you really feel a calling to do it, whatever 'it' might be, then know that you are supported in your efforts, you are not alone.

Anyway, in the unlikely event that things didn't turn out as you had hoped, what would be the cost of failing? Often it's just time and perhaps a loss of face – another tip for you:

Reframe 'Failure' as feedback and look for the positive.

As many people know, Edison took over 10,000 attempts before successfully inventing the light bulb and saw each 'failed' attempt as having discovered one more way that didn't work. Anthony Robbins went bankrupt before reinventing himself and becoming possibly the most successful inspirational speaker on the planet. Study the biographies of people like Joe Vitale, Richard Branson, Amitabh Bachchan, Pat O'Bryan, Oprah Winfrey and many others; you'll find that in most cases, they suffered setbacks on the way. As discussed in the first part of the book, reframing is a very useful technique to develop. Put simply, it's looking for the silver lining in the cloud, looking for the positive in a seemingly negative situation. To address one common misconception, reframing is not denial. Remember, there is no one definitive map. You create your own reality, based upon your perception. That's another way of saying that you choose what an event means to you. All too often, we feel a loss of control or believe that we have no choices. That's partly because we see things in a single frame of reference, but by reframing, we re-affirm to ourselves that we have options and choices, that we have some control over our lives.

2. Fear of Success/It takes so much energy to succeed

Whilst some people are afraid of failure, others are afraid of the success, or of their perception of the price that they will have to pay for their success.

Competing Internal Programs

Typically, people with such fears undermine the possibility of success by having competing internal programs. While I prefer the term 'competing internal programs', in psychology these are often called 'self-sabotage programs'. Whichever you choose to call them, they are defined as thoughts that become behaviors that undermine a person's therapy, healing or success in reaching their goals.

This is because any non-conscious state or 'force' can easily dominate all the conscious efforts we make. It often reflects circular logic or self-fulfilling prophecies confirming the person's self-defeat.

Competing internal programs were often originally intended by the non-conscious to protect us at a time when it thought our survival was in jeopardy. Unfortunately, often many years later, that same program is still running when not only is there is no longer any need for it, but it now hinders our development.

We need to understand that this undermining of our stated goals is not deliberate; it is not a manifestation of a lack of desire, skills, knowledge or effort. Rather, there's something inside us that is stronger than our conscious desire to heal and it sabotages our efforts. Sabotage Programs can affect every dimension of a person's being, physical, mental, emotional or spiritual.

Behaviors stemming from competing internal programs are most recognizable as an internal 'tug-of-war'. An example is the client who wishes to lose weight but rewards each loss with a chocolate binge!

This conflict between stated aim and our behavior can leave us feeling very frustrated; we feel trapped in a situation we desperately want to change, but can't. Some people give up trying, saying that theirs is a special case. In other cases, during a coaching session, a client offers up solutions that appear to be credible, whilst the real issue remains unaddressed.

We all have competing internal programs and when we are behaving based on one of these programs that are rooted in attitudes and beliefs that are false or distorted, we often feel that it is not 'our self' that is responsible for our sabotaging actions. We feel betrayed by this emotional defense system, not understanding why we are undermining ourselves so actively.

3. Poverty or Scarcity Consciousness

When we were growing up, most of us were told when we were growing up that we should not be greedy or selfish. We may also have been brought up to believe that the world has only a limited amount of resources, that there's not enough to go round so we're being selfish if we succeed. John Kehoe (1992) summed it up when writing:

"Imprint these four prosperity beliefs into your unconscious mind:

- It's an abundant Universe.
- Life is fun and rewarding.
- Staggering opportunities exist for me in every aspect of my life.
- Having lots of money is good. It is my responsibility to be successful."

There is nothing greedy or unspiritual about having money; it's what you do with it that matters. The negative aspect is greed, keeping it all for yourself, wanting money for money's sake. The positive is all the good you can do with the money you earn - it's difficult to make a difference in the world without earning the money first.

4. **Life is hard with little reward**

You are wealthy right now! We all have riches, whether family, friends, place of worship, financial wealth, work, organizations we belong to etc. The thing is, only financial wealth pays the bills. You can choose to build your riches, including your financial wealth, or you can undermine yourself with poverty consciousness and believing you are unworthy to have money. It's up to you! Yes you have to put the effort in, and the reward is commensurate with the effectiveness of the effort you put in. Note the subtle difference – I didn't write that the 'reward is commensurate with the effort you put in', but with the 'effectiveness of the effort.' There's a huge difference!

The distinction is simple – effectiveness means doing the right things (as opposed to efficiency which means doing things in the best way), so are you being effective? In other words, is everything you do aimed at living your dream? If the answer is 'no!', then yes, life can appear to be hard with little reward.

True success never diminishes someone else, it is never selfish. Make sure that you never allow yourself to be jealous of someone else's success. Instead, see it as proof that if they can succeed, so can you! As well as the direct benefits your service provides, there are also the indirect benefits; you spend the fruits of your success, creating profit for others, contributing to the economy as those people in turn spend their greater profits and so on.

5. **Having a closed mind**

This is typified by phrases such as "There are already so many books out there", "That won't work for me because…", "It won't work in the current economic climate", "That might work for most people, but I'm different/my situation is different", and so on.

A closed mind is another way of saying that "My perception of the world is right and is the only valid one." It actually becomes a self-reinforcing, vicious circle; your perception is your reality, as we will see later. If you continue to believe that it's 'Your way or the highway', then you are right, it won't work for you; a closed mind closes down its options.

6. Money is unspiritual

You can be spiritually rich and financially prosperous – spirit and matter are not separate. Indeed, one of the reasons that you are here on earth is to live your dream to the benefit of everyone, including you! Think of it this way. As you reap the rewards of your success, think about all of the causes you'll then be free to support, to invest in! The more money you make, the greater the causes you can invest in! Money is unspiritual if we allow it to manage us. However, if we manage it, and use it to enjoy life and to fund great causes, it becomes a spiritual tool. To put it another way – how can you donate to worthwhile causes if you don't have the money with which to donate?

7. I am unworthy/nothing good ever happens to me

This is one I can really identify with; for a long time, due to an overheard conversation that I misunderstood, I believed that my younger brother was more intelligent than me and that nothing good ever happened, or would happen, to me. This was exacerbated by my mother's death, which served to reinforce the belief that only bad things happen to me.

It's a dangerous mind-set to have, because anything to the contrary is discounted or ignored. Of course, lots of good things happened to me, but because that didn't fit my model of the world at the time, I ignored them or found an excuse to invalidate them.

8. Nothing I do is good enough

People who live in victim mode often believe this. If this applies to you, my question for you is what are you using as your comparison? Good enough compared to what or whom? And look at your belief... nothing? Have you never produced a good result at anything? At some stage in your life, you must have succeeded at something. So you can get good results. This means that the belief is false. Time to reprogram yourself!

9. My failure is a result of bad karma from a past life

If you believe that you carry 'bad karma' into this life from a past life, think of this: it can't have been that bad as you were allowed to incarnate here so think of it as being given a second chance to take whatever actions are necessary to succeed. And part of that second chance may well be to cancel any 'negative karmic energy' that you believe you carry by giving. Make it a regular practice to give money to whoever inspires you, or whoever you consider to be worthy of it and you will find that any karmic residue will be dissolved and that you will attract more money, a proportion of which you can give away and so on. Get more, give more, get even more, give even more and so it goes on!

10. God will provide so I don't need to do anything

God/the Universe/Spirit are available to help you if asked, but they won't do it for you; as I've said before, you have to play your part. My wife has a great expression "Trust God but lock the car doors when you park."

BIBLIOGRAPHY

1. Cherry, K., n.d. *About.com Psychology.* [Online] Available at: http://psychology.about.com/od/personalitydevelopment/a/emotionalintell.htm [Accessed 22 August 2013].
2. Coaching Leaders Ltd 2012, 2012. *Coaching Leaders.* [Online] Available at: http://www.nlpwebstore.com/free-downloads/what-is-appreciative-inquiry [Accessed 22 August 2013].
3. Cooperrider, D.L. & Whitney, n.d. *A Positive Revolution in Change: Appreciative Inquiry (Draft).* [Online] Available at: http://appreciativeinquiry.case.edu/uploads/whatisai.pdf. [Accessed 22 August 2013]
4. Duckworth, A. L., Steen, T. A. & Seligman, M. E., 2005. Positive Psychology in Clinical Practice. *Annual Reviews Clinical Psychology,* Volume 1, pp. 629-651.
5. Frankl, V. 2004 *Man's Search For Meaning* s.i.: Rider
6. Fromm, E. 1956. *The Art of Loving* s.l.: Harper & Row
7. Kaptchuk, T., Kelley, J., Conboy, L. & al, e., 2008. Components of placebo effect: randomised controlled trial in patients with irritable bowel syndrome. *British Medical Journal,* 336(7651), pp. 999-1003.
8. Kehoe, J., 2008. *Mind Power Into the 21st Century: Techniques to Harness the Astounding Powers of Thought.* s.l.:Zoetic Books.
9. Kelley, T. M., 2003. *Health Realization: A Principle-Based Psychology of Positive Youth Development.* Detroit, Human Sciences Press, Inc.

10. Litvin, R. & Chandler, C., 2013. *The Prosperous Coach: Increase Impact for You and Your Clients.* s.l.: Maurice Basset.
11. Mayer, J. D. et al., n.d. *Emotional Intelligence Information.* [Online] Available at: http://www.unh.edu/emotional_intelligence/index.html [Accessed 22 August 2013].
12. Rees-Evans, D. A. K., 2011. *Threeprinciplestraining.com.* [Online] Available at: http://www.threeprinciplestraining.com/files/dissertation_final.pdf [Accessed 22 August 2013].
13. Segal, J. & Smith, M., 2013. *Helpguide.org.* [Online]. Available at: http://www.helpguide.org/mental/eq5_raising_emotional_intelligence.htm [Accessed 22 August 2013].
14. Seligman, M. E. & Csikszentmihalyi, M., 2000. Positive Psychology: An Introduction. *American Psychologist,* 55(1), pp. 5-14.
15. Stavros, J & Hinrichs, G., 2009. *The Thin Book of SOAR. Building Strengths-Based Strategy.* s.l.: Thin Book Publishing Co
16. SydneyBanks.org, 2010. *SydneyBanks.org.* [Online]. Available at: http://www.sydneybanks.org/ [Accessed 22 August 2013].
17. Wagner, D 2013 *Expert Success - more Money, More Time, More Purpose* s.l.: Expert Success LL

Printed in Great Britain
by Amazon.co.uk, Ltd.,
Marston Gate.